To ARNOld
the "GO-TO GUY"
WHEN IT COMES to
helping ASPIRING
SPEAKERS.

MAKING COMPANIES WORK

7 Keys To Higher Profits, Happier Employees, & More Satisfied Customers

Alan Stafford

ePlanet Publishing, Inc.
Charlotte, North Carolina

ePlanet Publishing, Inc.
10925 David Taylor Drive, Suite 100
Charlotte, North Carolina 28262
Ph: 704-792-9092   Fax: 704-788-6694
www.eplanetpublishing.com

The information in this book is intended to be educational, informative, and maybe even entertaining. Neither the publisher nor the author guarantees that your company will be more successful, that your sales will increase, or that you will earn more profit. Use this information at your discretion. The results are up to you. The author and publisher are in no way liable for your use or failure to use any of the provided information.

Stafford, Alan.
   Making companies work : 7 keys to higher profits, happier employees, and more satisfied customers / Alan Stafford.

   p. ; cm.

   ISBN-13: 978-0-9793818-0-5
   ISBN-10: 0-9793818-0-0

1. Management. 2. Leadership. 3. Customer services. I. Title.

HD31 .S73 2007
658.4   2007904568

10 9 8 7 6 5 4 3 2 1

Making Companies Work: First Printing 2007
Printed in the United States of America
Cover Design by Pamela Delaney

For more information about bulk pricing for corporations, associations, and universities please contact the publisher at 1-866-200-3888, or email bulk@eplanetpublishing.com.

Alan speaks on topics of critical importance to business. For more information about Alan's speaking programs visit www.staffordspeakingconsulting.com.

Alan also does in-house training and workshops on leadership, organizational development, and customer service. For more information about Alan's site visits and consulting visit www.staffordspeakingconsulting.com.

To order copies of this book for associates and friends, please visit www.makingcompani+swork.com.

Give this book to everyone in your organization. Contact Alan at alan@staffordspeakingconsulting.com to see how this book can be customized for maximum impact on your organization.

To my good friend and mentor,
Arnold Sanow,
*for helping me with the most challenging part
of this book:*

writing page one.

Preface

What this book is about

Companies today are looking for that Magic Bullet...that hip new management technique, that "paradigm shift" that will transform their businesses into industry darlings with little effort by the companies. It's so appealing to turn to a management guru, a buzzword, or a new book to find the answers to the challenges of running a business. But the reality is that the fundamentals of business success have already been proven in thousands of companies across the country. This book covers what works.

The ideas in this book are not new. But in too many companies, they seem to have been forgotten. So, in a sense, this is a back-to-basics book. The ideas within are intended to spark discussion in stockholder meetings, boardrooms, executive suites, and employee meetings.

We are seeing the continuing trend toward non-owner executives running corporations. Founders and owners are driven by their purpose. They want to build the better mousetrap or serve an unserved market. To the founder of a company profit is important, but it is not the reason he started the business. On the other hand, today's CEOs are hired managers-sometimes called hired guns-brought in primarily to make money for the company. They do not have a long history with the company. They do not share the founder's passion. And they will probably not spend the rest of their lives with the company.

Under the circumstances, it's not surprising that the emphasis on money results in the CEOs emphasis on personal gain. We're also seeing a growing disconnect between the interests of the CEOs and the interests of the employees, the customers, and even the shareholders. What corporations need from their CEOs is leadership. What the corporations get all too often is Greedership: the tendency for some CEOs to get paid millions of dollars regardless of performance, then to walk away with millions more in severance even though the company is worse off than before they arrived.

As companies have grown larger, the dollar amounts involved have grown larger as well. A billion dollars isn't what it used to be. In the United States alone, there are more than 1200 public companies whose gross revenues exceed one billion dollars each year. So paying a CEO 10, 50, or even 210 million dollars seems insignificant when compared to total company revenues. But dollars aside, such largesse hurts companies in other ways.

With the financial stakes so high, some CEOs get preoccupied with the short-term financial results of a company. They make decisions which may temporarily boost the stock price, but hurt the company in the long run. It doesn't matter to them because they'll be gone in a few years. All that matters is the next quarter's results-and their own stock options. They cut costs in the wrong places and cut jobs indiscriminately. And, they rush to adopt every new management fad that promises to be the quick fix or the answer to all the company's problems.

This preoccupation with the short-term distracts CEOs from the true purpose of the company: serving customers wants and needs in a way that produces profit. This preoccupation also reduces employees to disposable assets that can be added or dismissed-whatever it takes to hit the numbers.

This book identifies the major issues within the many dysfunctional companies in America. It is not intended to be an indictment of all businesses. Instead, the book attempts to offer strategies and practices that businesses can employ to make their companies work better. Most people still work for someone else. And more than half of all households own stock in American corporations. What's good for business IS good for America.

I have deliberately chosen to write this book in a casual, reader-friendly style. Academic texts are read mostly by academics. I intend this book to be read by CEOs, C-level executives, senior executives, middle managers, team leaders, directors, stockholders, and even employees. More than that, it is my hope that the management keys I have provided will be embraced and implemented in businesses everywhere.

What this book can do for you and your company

This book will show you the mistakes other companies have made. Perhaps you will see your company in these pages and will be inspired to adopt some of the ideas in this book.

You will learn why most mission and vision statements are a waste of time and paper. You will also have a guide to follow should you decide to write or rewrite your own mission and vision statements.

You will learn the difference between purpose and profit, and why both are critical to the success of your organization.

You will have a new framework for developing leadership in your company. This information applies to everyone in the company, not just the CEO.

You will see that downsizing and layoffs are short-term solutions that do not fix the underlying problems.

You will have a new appreciation for the importance of customer service. You will be able to better communicate this to everyone in the company.

Finally, you will have the 7 Keys to Higher Profits, Happier Employees, and More Satisfied Customers. Revisit these every day. And reinforce every day with everyone the purpose and mission of the organization.

My purpose

My purpose for writing this book was to help companies across America earn higher profits while creating happier employees and more satisfied customers. All three come as a package. A company is not truly successful unless it has all three.

Acknowledgements

As an author, it is easy to feel that you are the one doing all the work. But as I completed this project, I was amazed by the details involved and impressed by the efforts of all the people who helped make this book a reality.

First, my thanks to Arnold Sanow. He got me moving on the project and was the inspiration for the title.

I'm also grateful to Jim Hamilton for providing some of the research and for helping with the writing of the book.

I'd also like to acknowledge Karen Colvin who designed the interior layout of the book. She patiently performed edit after edit to get the look just right and make the book an attractive, easy read.

Finally, my thanks to the staff of my publisher, ePlanet Publishing, Inc. I now have a better understanding of all the elements that go into the printing, publishing, and promoting of a commercial, hard-cover book.

Table of Contents

Chapter One

Celebrity CEOs

There is a serious problem with the way many American businesses are being run. Corporate profits are strong, but there is an underlying uneasiness throughout the country. Some have called it a crisis of leadership. Once, CEOs were seen as business role models: shrewd business chieftains who created jobs, increased shareholder value, and helped make our country more competitive. Now, they are largely seen as selfish prima donnas who eliminate jobs, weaken companies, and send overseas our production as well as our intellectual capital. We have transitioned from an era of leadership to an era of Greed-ership. This Greedership is at its most outrageous when CEOs get paid tens of millions of dollars while leaving their companies worse off than before.

Sooner or later, the Hollywood mentality of glitz and glamour, of style over substance, was bound to show up in the boardrooms of corporate America. After all, the prevalence of prima donnas and over-inflated egos has long been a part of the entertainment industry, and has become a part of our political culture as well. Even professional athletes and team owners buy in to the notion that sports are more about entertainment than sport and competition. So it shouldn't be surprising that boards of directors began to define leadership as celebrity as they scrambled to look for the stars, the celebrated and charismatic wonder workers, of the corporate world. It became a game of one-upsmanship as company after company fell all over themselves trying to snag the shining stars of the corporate universe.

Undoubtedly, one of the first of these *superstar* CEOs was Lee Iacocca. Even though Iacocca was a successful senior executive at Ford Motor Company, he was given a pink slip in 1978. His reaction to being fired from the second largest American automaker was to join Chrysler Corporation, the third largest. In one of his first acts as CEO of a nearly bankrupt Chrysler, Iacocca went to Washington, where he managed to secure a loan guarantee from Congress. With the additional capital Chrysler started a remarkable rebound. Over the next twelve years, Lee Iacocca's fame rose as Chrysler's recovery continued. His autobiography (written with William Novak) became the number one best-selling non-fiction hardback of 1983-84. Few would dispute that Iacocca was an astute businessman and a forward-thinking "car man". But many would also agree that the loan guarantee and Chrysler's comeback were more the result of his personality and prominence.

Perhaps prompted by Iacocca's success and the remarkable comeback of Chrysler, company boards of directors all over the nation began to envision a business model that consisted solely of hiring a high-profile celebrity CEO. Otherwise rational corporate directors failed to comprehend that a business model based on a single individual is no model at all. Then along came Jack Welch. When he became CEO of General Electric, the company had a market value of $14 billion dollars. Three years after he left the company, GE's market value had risen 28-fold to $410 billion. Upon Welch's retirement, his $4 million annual salary turned into an $8 million annual pension. But, the important point here is that his financial reward was the result of his amazing track record at GE. His compensation also was insignificant compared to the increase in shareholder value during his tenure.

However, as other boards and shareholders tried to copy the successes of Chrysler and GE, they got it completely backwards.

They didn't see that generous executive compensation was the reward for, and not the driver of, increased stock prices. As boards of directors all across corporate America looked on, they seemed to miss the point entirely. The formula for success, they reasoned, was hiring a celebrity CEO, paying him an exorbitant salary, and writing astronomical severance and retirement clauses into his or her contract. In short: pay before performance. Even the headline grabbing flame-out of "Chainsaw Al" Dunlap at Sunbeam Corp. did little to detract from the starry-eyed belief that a celebrity head of a corporation was the key to success.

More recently, women celebrity CEOs have made headlines after rising to the heavens before becoming spectacular supernovas. Carly Fiorina, then head of Hewlett-Packard Corporation, was paid an annual salary of over $8 million during her tenure while she made changes to the company that resulted in both successful market share increases and profit threatening losses. Her most celebrated action involved the acquisition of Compaq computers. For a while, it seemed like a shrewd move as HP/Compaq computers moved to the top of the PC market. However, as you might have expected, Dell and other competitors did not fold their tents and give up in the face of the newer, bigger HP. Instead they redoubled their efforts and within a short time, HP computers saw stock prices down 19% and market share stagnant at number 2 worldwide. Although named to *Time Magazine's* Top 100 CEOs in 2004, Fiorina was ousted the following year when the HP Board came to grips with the reality that stardom on the top floor was doing little for profits on the ground floor. Under the terms of her severance contract, Fiorina was paid an astonishing $21 million- a sum that HP had to fork over regardless of slumping sales.

Another highly touted and highly paid celebrity CEO, Gary Wendt, left GE after growing its Financial Services division to the point of accounting for 40% of GE's corporate revenue. Even though Jack Welch had sought Wendt's resignation when Wendt's celebrity was tarnished by a spectacularly public divorce, the publicity only further enhanced his qualifications for celebrity status. When the directors of Conseco, a troubled insurance company, looked around for a superstar savior, Wendt was at the top of their list. He was a high profile executive, and he was available. Offered a $45 million sign-on bonus as well as a compensation package that was rumored to be in the $200 million range, Wendt stepped in. His celebrity did, in fact, see Conseco's stock rise because of investor expectations. But star power lasts only so long. Two years later, the company was still in Titanic mode. Wendt stepped down, and Conseco was further saddled with millions of dollars of payouts to Wendt for the rest of his life.

Tyco International was flying high when its celebrity CEO was pictured on the cover of *Business Week* magazine. He was touted as the "Most Aggressive CEO" in the country and was held up as a role model for executives everywhere. When it later turned out that L. Dennis Kozlowski was using company funds for his own lavish living, the picture changed. A subsequent government investigation ended with his conviction for fraud amounting to some $600 million of the company's revenue. Tyco International was left holding a bag of debt while suffering public disgrace and ridicule.

Then, there was the much touted appointment of Michael Ovitz as head of a struggling Walt Disney Company in 1995. Fourteen months later with no tangible successes, Ovitz was dismissed with a severance that cost Disney nearly $140 million. One-seventh of a billion dollars paid not as a reward for performance, just paid so he would go away.

This list could go on and on with examples of spectacular failures of celebrity CEOs in the corporate world in recent years. The above examples, however, are enough to paint a sobering picture of the failure that has almost always results from thc flawed idea that a celebrity at the top can change the fortunes of a struggling company. By now it should be apparent that celebrity is no predictor of success. This cult of personality is more often than not damaging to corporate performance, employee morale, customer relations, and stockholder value. As a management strategy, hiring senior executives based on their celebrity has no legitimate place in sound business practices.

It should be noticed that there is a major difference between hired CEOs who come to the table with a certain celebrity and charisma and CEOs who have become celebrated through their own efforts, building their own companies. The difference is that these CEOs with their excellent business models are significant, if not major, stockholders in their companies—usually the founders and quite often the majority owners of the companies. Their business acumen and demonstrated success is what made them celebrities rather than some kind of jet set presence in the glitzy world of entertainment. They are totally unlike the hired gun CEOs who own a miniscule interest in the company they are supposed to fix. Founders' celebrity is the result of their success. They are not expected to be successful because they are famous.

> *"Executives who leave their companies worse off than before still walk away with severance packages of $20 million to $140 million."*

People like Bill Gates, Warren Buffet, Rupert Murdock, Steve Jobs, and Donald Trump can be classified as self-made celebrities. They are not hired guns brought into their companies in the desperate hope that they will save the day. The motivation of self-made celebrity CEOs is to make their businesses successful. This is quite different from the hired CEOs whose compensation packages show no correlation between their perceived celebrity status and any financial performance. Steve Jobs of Apple Computers is an outstanding example of a celebrity who became famous for his vision and innovation. Jobs is always shifting the attention away from himself and onto the products his company produces. Our criticism of celebrity CEOs is focused on the senior executives whose primary motivation is self-promotion and self-aggrandizement.

Herein is the crux of the problem: the lack of correlation between performance and employment packages for the celebrity CEOs. What a difference it might make, say, if the contractual severance package written into a new CEOs agreement stipulated that the payout would be regulated by the value of company stock at the time of the separation. An alternative might be an option strike price that is a 6-month rolling average rather than an atypical spike in stock price on a given day. Severance pay could also be based on the eminently sensible notion that you should be rewarded in proportion to the increase in profitability during your tenure. Under the prevailing system of executive compensation there is a disconnect between pay and performance-both current pay and severance pay. Executives who leave their companies worse off than before still walk away with severance packages of $20 million to $140 million. So we have the amazing spectacle of companies going downhill, and yet having to pay millions to people who participated-or even led-the decline. The bottom line is simply that the companies were in trouble before the celebrity CEO was hired. When he or she leaves after having failed to create any turnaround, the companies are in worse shape than they were when they started. They are worse off than before and are now saddled with future payouts that further weaken their companies. This is what passes for corporate governance today.

What actually happens when these celebrity CEOs come on board anyway? First of all, there is almost always an immediate disconnect between the CEO and the employees of the company. It's difficult to imagine employees, concerned about their own futures in a company that is on the verge of bankruptcy, welcoming an imperious CEO whose fantastic employment contract is written up with great fanfare in the nation's newspapers. In many cases, the hard working employees have foregone pay raises or any kind of recognition for jobs well done. Depending on their own notoriety to raise the value of the company's bottom line, these new superstar CEOs have little need to increase company intracommunication or develop time tested methods of teamwork.

The boards of directors who orchestrated the hiring of these celebrities have actually worked against themselves, abetting the discontent within the companies. It is pie in the sky to expect one person to be the magic bullet that turns the desert into green pastures. No single human being can possibly accomplish such a pipe dream. It takes the dedicated cooperation of the entire workforce within the company. Most often, key employees within the organization begin to drift away in the wake of the celebrity hype. The only thing that works is an upper management that stays connected to every employee in the company. The celebrity CEO almost universally seems to be oblivious to this simple truth. The genuine superstar CEOs are largely invisible, staying as much as possible out of the limelight, preferring instead to see that the spotlight stays centered on the company itself.

To further illustrate the point, let's look at the opposite of the celebrity CEO. In early 1980 a new corporation was born which was (at the time) the largest corporate spin-off in American corporate history. At the helm of the new Valero Energy Corporation was a visionary, Bill Greehey. It is part of company legend that Greehey worked for a salary of $1 per year as he led the San Antonio, Texas, based company through success after success over a quarter-century. In 2007 Valero had moved up to 16th on the Fortune 500 list of America's largest public companies.

Aside from Greehey's astute mergers and acquisitions, all of which were related to the oil and gas industry, his philosophy of involving the entire workforce in the steady growth of the company created unprecedented employee loyalty. When Greehey stepped down at the end of 2005, employees were virtually unanimous in singing his praises and telling how his corporate business practices had enriched their lives.

Was Bill Greehey a superstar? In the sense that he guided an infant company to the peak of its oil and gas industry, most certainly. In the sense of being wined and dined amidst the flashing bulbs of the paparazzi to satisfy his own ego, certainly not. When he retired, his employees shared a sense of loss. That is a far cry from the many stories of employees literally dancing in the streets when an aloof celebrity CEO is given his walking papers.

Sound Management and Genuine Leadership

Celebrity figureheads tend to alienate the employees, and company morale suffers. It is amazing that otherwise astute company directors could have ever had the lapses that convinced them of the value in hiring these shooting stars. In effect, they seemed to expect a showman to be the magic bullet that would turn their companies around. In most cases, the end result is only an expensive and acrimonious severance accompanied by bad press that does nothing for stock values of the companies involved.

At Valero Energy Corporation, sound management and genuine leadership were seen as the foundation for its remarkable growth. Fundamental to its business strategy was a willingness to change to meet existing business conditions. Mergers and acquisitions for the company were moves within its own field of expertise and, according to Greehey, always improved the salaries and working conditions of the people in the companies they acquired.

In fact, development of a corporate culture that involved all employees from lowest to highest echelons was central to Greehey's vision of how best to run a company. He saw to it that if he got a bonus, every single employee of the company received a bonus simultaneously. It was his "employees first" attitude that created one of the most successful corporate cultures in the business world.

Valero did not go about willy-nilly making acquisitions just for the sake of the publicity and glory for some celebrity CEO. To Valero, acquisitions amounted to business growth only when such additions could mutually benefit both companies involved. In 1981, Valero acquired an interest in a small crude refining company in Corpus Christi, Texas, which eventually demonstrated the company's and Greehey's foresight. That small company had developed a process for production of high-grade fuel from low-grade crude oil and is today a large, state-of-the-art facility. It produces clean-burning fuel from bottom-of-the-barrel crude which can be purchased at a significant discount compared to sweet crude. Greehey saw the potential for that process and correctly anticipated the future supply problems for the refining industry.

By 1997, Valero had become, through careful and well thought out acquisitions, the largest independent refining company on the coast of the Gulf of Mexico. By the end of 1998, another strategic acquisition made Valero the nation's second largest refining company with an output capacity of 735,000 barrels per day. By 2000, Valero had expanded to the West Coast and entered the retail business under its own brand, Valero. By 2005, Valero had become the largest refiner in all of North America with a combined output of nearly three and a half million barrels per day.

None of Valero's acquisitions were done for the media hype or for lining the pockets of investment bankers. It was steady growth under sound management and genuine leadership. It is a business model that works rather than a Hollywood fantasy built on hype.

Glamour and Glitz Are Not a Sustainable Business Model

In Chapters 2 and 3 we will cover the reasons most mergers and acquisitions do not work. But it is important at this point to note the correlation between the celebrity CEO and the merger and acquisition mania that inevitably follows. The celebrity CEO does not come to the position as a person of great loyalty to the company. In many cases, he or she may not even have a comprehensive overview of the company at all. Even CEOs who have achieved celebrity status through their efforts in growing companies in which they had a significant interest have failed miserably to be effective when they moved on to new companies. Their primary interest in their new positions seems to be generally in lining their own pockets. What else could explain their penchant for insulating their compensation from their new companies' performance? In cases where out-and-out fraud was not involved such as at Tyco, the hired hand wonder boy of celebrity status generally appears to be looking out for increasing his celebrity status rather than any serious benefit to the company.

What the celebrity CEO brings to the company is generally not fresh insights into the business. What he or she brings is a spotlight that is rarely on the company and consistently on the CEO who is always ready for a close-up photo and an interview. It is a far cry from the likes of the late Sam Walton who wore ordinary work clothes and drove an old car even at the time he was the wealthiest man in the world. The celebrity prefers wearing designer clothes, revels in being seen in all the "in" places, and surrounds himself with sycophants who are constantly massaging his or her ego.

Celebrity CEOs also seem to believe their own press hype, even if no one else does. Journalists unwittingly encourage this by overstating the impact of a CEO on a company's performance. The reality is that, over the years, most corporate successes and failures are due to external influences. Changing market conditions, changing political environments, even changing weather all influence the modern corporation far more than does the chief executive officer. We all recognize this when a company is in trouble. Business writers, elected officials, and the executives themselves hold the senior managers blameless. Gosh, it wasn't their fault. But whenever the company does well, whenever profits or stock prices are up, the CEO takes the credit. And we all nod our heads up and down in agreement and cheer.

Moreover, as a result of all that favorable media attention, the CEOs find themselves basking in the sunshine of public and political approval. They are wined and dined, held up as shining examples, called on to speak at important functions, treated with royal deference wherever they go, surrounded by every luxury, and sought out for advice. It is no wonder that people caught up in such adoration fall victim to their own overvalued self worth. When the bubble bursts in two or three years time, those celebrities luxuriate in their unwarranted severance packages and maintain that they had it right all the time—the boards of directors just didn't "get it."

The big losers in such ego trips, however, are the stakeholders including the company employees who wondered from the beginning what their boards of directors were thinking when these outrageous hirings were made. Employees typically have little or no say in the hiring of senior management. Yet it is the employees-and stockholders-who pay the biggest price for a bad executive hire. Stockholders can lose money; employees lose jobs and more. In theory, the Directors represent the stockholders. Perhaps we need a system that gives the employees a voice in who leads them.

Even among CEOs who tend to maintain a low profile like the late Ken Lay of Enron, the heady experiences of associating with Presidents and Congressmen, being named to positions of honor, receiving kudos and accolades from communities, and receiving flattering press coverage, tend to cause CEOs to overvalue themselves and undervalue the contributions of countless employees who really make the system work. The saddest part of it all is that the CEOs walk away with millions while the employees watch helplessly as their pensions, their benefits, and even their jobs disappear.

The Model Simply Does Not Work

Historically, the appointment of a celebrity to lead a troubled company simply has not worked. Usually there is a brief period of exhilaration when the announcement of the new CEO is made. Stock prices may even take a sudden jump after being in a major slump for some time. After a brief respite, however, when little progress is evidenced by the addition of the new celebrity, the stock prices fall again and a general malaise descends over the corporation. Employee morale erodes further. Often, the brightest managers and key personnel jump ship. Furthermore, the decision of the board of directors to hire the celebrity sends the wrong message to the employees. If the new CEO is to be the savior of the company, why should the employees make any special effort on behalf of the company? Subliminally, they adopt the attitude of "why exert myself when our new superstar can do it all himself?" Their thinking is actually reasonable when you consider the miracle worker abilities attributed to the new CEO.

When the overblown expectations of the directors, shareholders, and employees turn into bitter disappointments, the celebrity CEO remains above it all, fully aware that he or she will not be a loser in the outcome. Eventually, the expected panacea becomes a bitter pill. The case of Gary Wendt at Conseco is a classic example of inflated expectations being reduced to harsh realities. There was excitement at first as Wendt's upbeat reports to investors caused Conseco's stock to rise dramatically. But when no significant improvement had occurred within the company after two years, Wendt walked away millions richer.

And even though Lee Iacocca's charisma and personality were effective in leading Chrysler out of crisis when he took the helm, he was far less effective in the needed rebuilding to prevent the same situation from happening again. The press tended to give Iacocca far too much credit for the change, playing down the many executives he brought over from Ford Motor Company who played pivotal roles in the resuscitation of Chrysler.

Nobody really believes in the fairy tale of the dashing prince riding in on a noble steed to rescue the damsel in distress. Then why do otherwise sensible company directors, the mass media, and the general public turn into star-struck acolytes at the very mention of a celebrity CEO? Stock prices surge, and approval beams from delighted faces. For a brief moment, belief is suspended and the dark clouds all have silver linings. Reality only returns when it is obvious that no one is going to live happily ever after in this fairy tale.

The bitter truth is that not only does such a model not work but, in reality, it is no model at all. Stockholders often see what boards of directors overlook. The very inclusion of shocking severance packages in celebrity contracts is a harbinger of failure. The exorbitance of salaries (Ken Lay is reported to have drawn $42.7 million a year) is the antithesis of teamwork and mutual prosperity. Guaranteed multimillion dollar employment contracts are symptomatic of a troubled company sliding further downhill. In almost every case, there is an executive who lacks the passion and dedication to have the company succeed because he or she is insulated from the result. The problem lies not within an industry or sector. The problem is commonplace among American public companies. There is little, if any, connection between executive compensation and company performance. As a final insult, when a departing CEO leaves a company worse off than before, the company still has to pay millions to the CEO for presiding over its continued decline. Meanwhile, employees who do good work are fired. In most public corporations today, there is also no correlation between an employee's effort and whether he keeps his job. This corporate double-whammy is particularly destructive to a company and to the country's general work ethic.

In some cases, boards have reasoned that with a celebrity in the house, media attention will improve the company's visibility resulting in an increase in stock value and even net income. But time and again history has shown that whatever buzz is created by a celebrity CEO, the effect is short lived. Sustainable growth in earnings as well as steadily appreciating stock prices are the result of business basics: satisfying customers needs and wants, and doing it efficiently so that revenues exceed costs. Too late and far too often, everyone realizes that the celebrity CEO is not the company. He is an employee who shares in the responsibility of satisfying customers and increasing shareholder value. Unfortunately, it is rarely the ousted CEO who is disgraced when sent packing with a huge contract buyout. Nobody thinks the celebrity CEO was stupid to get a hefty, iron-clad severance clause written into his or her contract. Indeed, these CEOs are seen as sharp negotiators. The real astonishment is wondering what made the directors accept such a deal in the first place.

Other celebrity CEOs are given a blank check to cut bloody swaths throughout the company and make inexplicable acquisitions that do little more than saddle the company with more debt. After alienating many long time Ford Motor Company employees with his abrupt management style and making ill-advised mergers and acquisitions, Jacques Nasser was dismissed from Ford Motor Company. His free rein position at the once giant automobile manufacturer left Ford facing a drop in stock values that no one would have ever believed possible. Nevertheless, it was the company and not Nasser that bore the brunt of public scorn. Rather than putting effort into updating aging models such as the Taurus-considered a revolutionary design at the time of its introduction-Nasser chose a strategy of growth through acquisition. In fact, many models were discontinued in favor of the M&A strategy. Nasser's tenure not only failed to improve Ford's competitive position, but it would also be known for adding to the billions of dollars in additional losses for the car company that once was the largest and most successful in the world. Nevertheless, Nasser's celebrity status went unblemished. He ended up at an almost defunct Polaroid Corporation. A little over three years after Polaroid filed Chapter 11 bankruptcy, the former billion dollar company was sold for a mere $426 million. Nasser walked away with over $12 million personally while more than 4,000 retirees each received final checks for $47.00. They were also notified that their medical and life insurance programs were being discontinued. Nassar's story is further proof of the disconnect between executive compensation and company performance.

Real CEOs Don't Disappear (with money)

Hiring a high profile, celebrity CEO almost seems like the kiss of death. The celebrities come and go, most lasting less than five years. And usually, the companies are left worse off. Effective CEOs shun the spotlight and get down to the serious matters of effective business practices using proven business models. They also keep a sharp eye out for needed change in a rapidly changing world.

> *"Effective CEOs shun the spotlight and get down to the serious matters of effective business practices using proven business models."*

Pitney Bowes' CEO Michael J. Critelli is a great example of how an effective chief executive leads his company. Already a ten year veteran of the company, Critelli has guided the former "postage meter company" into the mainstream of the Internet age. Internet success stories such as eBay and Amazon.com use Pitney Bowes servers today. And the company is still thriving in a mail processing business that soothsayers of the modern age once predicted would go the way of the dinosaur. Traditional letters still find their way into mail boxes, but additional items such as CDs and pharmaceuticals-as well as an ever increasing volume of what the USPS euphemistically calls third-class bulk mail- now account for a large share of what passes through the nation's post offices. Pitney Bowes has grown with the times. It still has a large presence in mailing systems, a market in which it has always been a leader. There is a business model for you: change with the times but still grow in an industry where your company has proven expertise. How would the story be different at Ford Motor Company today if more emphasis had been placed on upgrading and improving the Taurus?

Critelli's success at expanding the fortunes of Pitney Bowes has not focused entirely on change or new markets. He credits much of the success to lessons learned at an early age about the emphasis on customer satisfaction being key to business success. To him, the consumer (whether a direct customer or not) is the key to success. To some it might seem like a nitpicking detail, but Critelli recognizes the fact that if a consumer is not satisfied with how he or she receives something in the mail, the sender will not be satisfied with the service or product manufactured or delivered by Pitney Bowes. What you see here, then, is a good basis for formulating a business plan. Consumers are concerned with what affects them personally. A strong business will work toward meeting those expectations. Consumers care little about the fame and status of the executive team. What consumers want is a positive customer experience. Simply stated, they want products that work and service that satisfies. Perhaps the question for directors should be "what can the prospective CEO do for our customers" instead of "what can we do for the new CEO?"

Critelli sees consumers in three categories as they react to change. He also observes that change in behavior and attitudes is far slower than technological change. Not everyone thinks new and improved is…well, an improvement. So while change for change's sake is unfounded, so is the stubborn resistance to change. It has to do with the reality of human psychology. When a business change occurs, a third of the public will accept it, another third will outright reject it, and the middle third will look at it with both anxiety and doubt. The same is true for employees. So how does that observation fit into a business plan? First, a bold plan does not waste time over those who resist change by total rejection. What's the point? The ones who accept change are the keys to successful change. A clever chief executive will look for ways to lead the undecided consumers (or employees) to join the top group of those who accept the change. But focusing on the resistant group is a losing strategy. Allowing the resistance to change to prevail may doom the entire corporation. Examples abound of companies that refused to acknowledge or adapt to changing conditions. Xerox, for example, developed and perfected dry-toner, plain-paper photocopying. For a while, it owned the market. Even today, many people still conflate the trade name Xerox with photocopying. Yet the company missed the development in digital technology to the extent that Xerox almost became extinct. Its leadership position was lost. Today, Xerox is just one of a number of players in the copier and printer markets.

Another criterion for a sound business model relates to direction of the company's efforts. If diversification through mergers and acquisitions is the strategy, then target companies should be evaluated not only for their contribution to the parent's overall diversification goals, but just as importantly for their competitive position within their industries. Why buy a company that has problems within its own industry? Bigger is not always better, especially when the two companies are in different industries or markets. In short, if a company is looking to grow through acquisition, it doesn't make much sense to buy another company having the same growth issues. Such a business model is in direct antithesis to the flashy acquisitions of companies that have no correlation with the buyer's current area of expertise. Those acquisitions make the headlines and, for a few fleeting moments seem like the coup of the century. When reality sets in, however, the foolishness of such moves becomes obvious. Interestingly, Steve Case, who was the mastermind of AOL's buyout of Time-

Warner, was later an outspoken advocate of dissolving that unprofitable business marriage.

A sound business model will concentrate on building teamwork within the existing framework of the company. As already observed, the hiring of a celebrity CEO generally has the effect of destroying whatever morale and teamwork existed before that unfortunate decision. A real CEO will set about to create the synergy that will bring all departments and divisions of a company together so that the entire organization is pulling together. A divided house is sure to fall.

At Pitney Bowes, perhaps the greatest accomplishment of Michael Critelli was tying executive compensation packages to company performance. That move alone would disqualify Critelli as a celebrity CEO, but boards of directors should sit up and take notice.

Another major difference between the celebrity CEO and the true leader lies in the investors the company cultivates. Investors attracted to the celebrity are more likely to be those who favor quick profits over long-term and steady growth. These are the investors who want the quick fix, even if it is detrimental to long-term, sustainable success. This emphasis on next quarter's results can give stock prices a short-term boost. And that's all the short-term speculator is looking for. But a year or two from now, the emphasis on short-term results can lead to disaster for the company and its loyal employees who find themselves suddenly on the street. Critelli favors the long-term investors who are aiming to have a good nest egg built up at retirement or when their children are ready for college. These value investors are then partners with management and will support a CEO who is in it for the long-term.

Hiring a celebrity CEO does have one benefit. A new CEO, especially an outsider, can bring a fresh outlook and a new way of thinking to a company. Employees tend to give a new celebrity CEO the benefit of the doubt when it comes to changes in the company. But, it's important to remember that successful change is the result of sound business practices carried out by motivated-even inspired-employees. Such inspiration is the definition of leadership. True inspiration does not last long in a cult of personality. At some point, poor company performance with resultant cuts in employee pay, benefits, or even jobs becomes apparent. Charisma is no substitute for profits. There's a saying in Texas that a pretender is "all hat, no cattle". The danger with celebrity CEOs is that when the employees realize that the CEO has no cattle, their motivation turns to disillusionment. Combine that disillusionment with a lack of solid business strategy and you soon see why celebrity CEOs can leave an organization far worse off than before. It's also mind-boggling that such an executive would end up better off while leaving the company worse off.

Critelli goes on to assert that change is easier when there is trouble than when things are going great for the company. People are more receptive to needed changes when they perceive them as moves to correct a problem. There is a great deal more resistance to change when business is good. Perhaps that explains the sometimes desperate rush to sign a celebrity CEO. Hiring the celebrity CEO becomes a sop to those who say "don't just sit there; do something. It is truly difficult at these times to remember that sometimes the old nothing is better than the new something.

Celebrity Is Not Taught in Business Schools

Good leadership with sound business models and charisma are not mutually exclusive terms. The best business plan is worthless without employees and staff motivated to carry it out. But the reverse is true as well. Motivation, especially enthusiasm by charisma is not sufficient either. Nor is it a substitute for sensible business practices. Business success requires both business skills and people skills. The danger with celebrity CEOs is the over reliance on the celebrity appeal. Charisma is important. But this charisma is the kind that appeals to people to perform for the good of the group and even for their own self interest. It is foolhardy- and a little bit arrogant-to expect people to perform, to help raise the company's stock price, so that the CEO can exercise his millions in stock options.

Business schools do not teach celebrity. They teach (or at least try to teach) leadership. Marketing departments teach company promotion, not self promotion. There is a reason for this. The reason is the recognition that no one works or succeeds alone. From the smallest company to the largest, it takes a team of people to deliver products and services to customers. The thinking that divides the company into management and employees, CEO and everyone else, eventually leads to the demise of the feeling that "we're all in this together". And that is precisely the problem with celebrity CEOs. They are not one of us. There is no correlation between their pay and performance and ours.

True leadership involves inspiring people to achieve more than they thought they could; to look beyond their own parochial interests and work for a larger good; and to work together to accomplish more than they could separately. Celebrity CEOs all too often succumb to the notion that they are a breed apart. They are entitled to be rewarded. So they may be hired, and they may be the bosses. But by our definition, they are not leaders. And they are not what American corporations need.

Keys to this Chapter

- 🔑 American business is becoming increasingly led by celebrity CEOs.

- 🔑 Leadership is being replaced by Greedership.

- 🔑 Many celebrity CEOs are being paid regardless of performance.

- 🔑 This disconnect of pay from performance usually results in diminished performance which results in decreasing shareholder wealth.

- 🔑 Layoffs and bankruptcies represent a failure of management.

- 🔑 Executives getting bonuses while employees get laid off is hurting America, damaging morale, and causing a decline in the work ethic.

Chapter Two

Merger Mania

Corporate buzzwords over the last twenty-odd years have included the redundant phrase "*mergers and acquisitions*" and its counterpart "*divestiture*." No matter how you cut the cake, a merger is an acquisition. There cannot be two CEOs, two top executives, or two bosses. The senior management personnel of one of the merged companies usually gets their walking papers or resigns in frustration not long after the ink dries on the final agreement. The reasoning is simple. If you want to increase revenue by merging the companies, what is the point of having duplicate sets of managers? Furthermore, the acquiring company imagines all sorts of cost savings, or so-called efficiencies from the merged companies. Redundancies and duplications will be eliminated. Costs will be reduced even though the combined revenues will be so much greater. At first glance, that thinking seems to make sense. Greater revenues with lower costs. What could be wrong with that?

No one seems to note or say out loud the obvious: if one set of duplicate managers is eliminated, then the surviving managers now have to manage twice as many employees. If the so-called redundant employees are fired, the remaining employees now have to do the work that both sets of employees did before. Let's assume that the acquiring company buys a second company. The combined companies will be 50% larger than the first company. Laying off a significant number of acquired employees will require the original employees to work 50% harder, faster, and more to keep up. If they could have done this before the merger, they would have. The very fact that the company bought another company means that the purchaser thought it could grow faster by acquisition than it could through internal growth.

After the dust of excitement and media blitz dies down following an acquisition, the next round of hoopla takes place when companies begin the process of divestiture, dumping the dogs that should not have been acquired in the first place. Of course each part of this cycle of merger-divestment, merger-divestment gets media coverage. In almost every case, the merger or divestment is hailed as a wise business move. Rarely does anyone look at the entire cycle to see that stockholders and employees would have been better off had the merger not taken place to begin with. Billions of dollars are involved in these acquisitions and divestitures. The need to divest a company of one of its acquisitions should raise the logical question: why was the acquisition made in the first place? Oddly, though, that is seldom the consideration. Everyone tends to assume that the CEO and board of directors have some kind of hidden wisdom that will strengthen the company revenues. In other words, most people and the media tend to think that these executives know what they are doing.

> *"Even the normally optimistic* **Economist** *magazine concedes that corporate mergers have something like an 83% failure rate."*

Even the normally optimistic *Economist* magazine concedes that corporate mergers have something like an 83% failure rate. So it seems strange that merger mania shows no sign of abating. In the face of so many mergers gone bad and the hasty divestitures that follow, what is it that keeps the momentum going? Actually, it appears to be like the mythical perpetual motion machine. It is the movement itself that clouds otherwise rational minds into thinking that the activity means progress.

The Selling Position

There may be several reasons a company decides to put itself on the market, but clearly none of those reasons arise out of a position of strength. Negative cash flow and dwindling market share account for most of the sales of businesses. Enter stage right the lawyers, investment bankers, and listing firms who are eager to facilitate these sales. It is not altruism at work. It is simply the huge profits that can be made in the form of hefty fees and commissions. Those are profits from commissions; not profits that accrue to stockholders.

When companies put themselves on the market for want of capital, the deal usually means that all other avenues for raising money have been exhausted. They have been unable to attract new investors or take out loans. These companies are looking at big layoffs and a myriad of other headaches that come with business failure. The temptation then is to sell the turkey and let the new owners be the layoff bad guys. What follows is a seller who has just pocketed a few million for himself rising up in righteous indignation sputtering, "If I had known they were going to lay off all these people, I would not have sold to them!" What planet is the guy from? Unless he is from Pluto, he had to know what was going to happen. Or, then again, maybe he did not because his own management ability was unsuccessful, necessitating the sale in the first place.

When it comes down to the ultimatum of sell or go out of business, selling the business will (1) provide some capital to the owner, and (2) avoid the problems associated with liquidating the business. The prospect of going out of business may not be an immediate threat, but the handwriting on the wall paints a dismal long-term picture. The seller may actually convince himself that a buyer—any buyer—can manage his company better than he could. That dubious proposition is more often than not accompanied by the willingness to sell to buyers who have absolutely no knowledge of the products or services of the selling company! The only consideration for the sale is whether or not the potential buyer has cash and/or financing for the deal.

Buyer Fever

The fever for acquisitions is often a symptom of ego on the part of the celebrity CEO. If the merger is big enough and flashy enough, the CEO will find his face staring back at him or her from the cover of a national news magazine. What a trip!   The CEO and the directors of the acquiring company feel a great sense of power. The wining and dining and media frenzy that accompanies such power moves is a heady experience. Everyone gets bedazzled by the size of the newly merged company and confuses revenues with margins.

Now, let's look at this one step at a time.   Revenue from acquisition rarely results in increased profit margins. What most mergers mean is that the new company is larger, and the combined revenues are greater. It does not follow that the new company is any more profitable. What matters is ROI, rate of return, profitability. The new company can become the largest in the world, but it's all for nothing if the company suffers losses. Rate of return is what attracts capital. Rate of return (risk adjusted) is what causes investors to favor one investment over another. Defining success in total sales dollars is a fool's game. Nevertheless, what usually happens is that the new owner gets-at best-the same rate of return from the new acquisition as he does in the parent company. Sales are greater in absolute dollars, but the merger does not raise the profit margin. The implication is clear—the buyer admits an inability to grow his or her own business by investing in it! Something is wrong with that picture. Why does a buyer think he or she can run a seller's business better than the seller did? For that matter, why does the seller think the buyer can run the business better than he could? This question is especially relevant when the acquired company is from an entirely different business sector or industry than the buying company.

A look at the track record of acquisitions over the past couple of decades bears out the fact that most of the time the fanciful expectations just did not pan out. Stellar among such acquisitions would possibly be the example of Mattel CEO Jill Barad's acquisition of The Learning Company for $3.6 billion in the spring of 1999. Scarcely sixteen months later, Mattel unloaded the company for $430 million. Imagine buying a house for $360,000 and selling it for $43,000. What happened? On the surface, Mattel toys and the child-based Learning Company seemed like a perfect fit. It certainly must have looked good to the investment bankers, lawyers, and CEO Barad herself. The reality was that toy company management had no expertise in publishing. Even a cursory look at mergers over the past two decades will show that most companies in the merger game have divested more than they have acquired.

Often, when mergers occur, the expected rise in shareholder value never materializes. The track record of CEO instigated mergers is not good. Either these CEOs should stay focused on their own companies, or at least turn away from the siren calls of the investment bankers who so often are the drivers of these bad deals. What followed after AT&T acquired NCR in 1991 is another example of an acquisition that was not made in heaven. After four years of financial loses instead of the predicted gains, NCR was turned loose from the acquisition by AT&T. What had looked like a great merger on paper failed to materialize. Out of those four years of struggle under the umbrella of AT&T came two major spin-offs—Lucent Technologies and the reemergence of NCR. The highly publicized merger of two seemingly complementary companies failed to meet expectations and quickly devolved into divestment. It is interesting to note that NCR, out from under the management of AT&T, went on from strength to strength under the direction of its own management team who were all experts in their particular field.

Another near disastrous acquisition that made headlines but produced nothing but headaches was GE's acquisition of NBC in 1986. Later, John F. Welch, Jr., CEO of GE, was sure he had sold NBC to Martin Davis of Paramount when suddenly the deal fell through as Davis angled for even greater stakes. It was not until 2004 that GE acquired 80% of Vivendi Universal with Vivendi retaining 20% and agreeing to manage NBC Universal. The cycle of mergers and spin-offs in the entertainment, publishing, and news industries during the 20 years is dizzying. However, not all mergers turn out so positive after a rocky start. The Union Pacific/Southern Pacific Railroad merger was supposed to facilitate rail movement and result in better rates for consumers. After the merger was completed in 1996, a maze of service disruptions and delivery delays plagued the new company and customer dissatisfaction soared. Citicorp's acquisition of Quotron Systems in the 1980s turned out so badly that some wags speculated that Citicorp might even consider paying someone to take the outdated Quotron off its hands. It finally sold for an undisclosed dollar amount.

More recently, Daimler-Benz has sold its Chrysler acquisition for approximately fifty cents on the dollar. GE has decided to sell its multi-billion dollar plastics unit. Gee, they both sounded like good ideas at the time, didn't they?

Literally hundreds of such examples could be cited to show that mergers and acquisitions are largely not the cure-alls they are touted as being. The M&A buzzword, synergy, sounds good to the ear, looks good on a paper proposal, but does not prove to be true in reality. The idea that two entities combined will have a greater result than the sum of their individual capabilities is especially ludicrous when the entities are not even remotely related in expertise. It is like saying that if a mule can pull a wagon at 3 miles per hour and a horse can pull a wagon at 5 miles per hour, then hitch them together and they will pull the wagon at 8 miles per hour. What actually happens is that the wagon moves only as fast as the slower animal. In many cases that is exactly what happens with corporations. The weaker company slows the faster company. The result is a bigger, slower company. Finally, the slower company is sold off with a resulting loss in stockholder value. In fact, it's about a twenty year cycle of merger-divestment. It continues to this day. Yet the merger mania shows no sign of letting up.

Merger Fallout

The old saw about there being "many a slip between the cup and the lip," applies well to the majority of mergers. The glowing expectations often turn into unwelcome surprises that were never anticipated in the excitement of the deal. Most of those unexpected surprises would not have occurred at all if greater attention had been paid to all possible details in the first place. There are a number of reasons that M&A's have, overall, turned out poorly since detailed records started being kept in the 1980's.

* **Integration** of the buying company and the selling company becomes difficult to achieve. Different companies even within the same industry, business, or service may have opposing ways of doing business which makes integration weak, if not impossible. There are usually different suppliers, different accounting systems, different IT infrastructure, and different HR policies. In the end, trying to integrate the companies often ends in failure and leads to hasty divestiture within 3 to 5 years of takeover. The AT&T/NCR short-lived merger is a good case in point.

  In the case of AT&T's acquisition of Cingular Wireless, integration problems arose over different billing and back-office systems. The resulting integration problems created a great deal of customer dissatisfaction. Competitors such as Verizon took note of the post-merger turmoil and made an extra effort to win over disgruntled customers from Cingular.

* **Employee morale** becomes a factor in all mergers. Following the merger of two companies, the differences in corporate cultures become exacerbated as two distinct environments attempt to assimilate each other. Typically, it is not an even exchange. There is a winner and a loser. And people resent losing. They also resist changing the way they've always done their jobs. Quite often this affects the employees of the seller's

company more than those of the buyer. Employee morale can plunge at these times causing a great deal of confusion and departure of key people. The employees of the acquired company can even go so far as to sabotage the merger in an attempt to regain their independence and autonomy.

For a merger to work well, emphasis needs to be placed on preparing the employees of both companies, and the plan must be ready for implementation the moment the merger takes place. It is just common sense that employees who arrive one morning to find that they now have a new boss, new company policies, and new procedures will be affected by all the change. In the case of acquisitions promulgated by celebrity CEOs and investment bankers, all too often the employees have never even been considered. The "what's in it for me?" attitude of the celebrity CEO does not translate into "what's in it for us?" of the employees.

What happens in any merger is the bringing together of two business cultures. Any co-mingling of cultures brings about its own set of problems whether socially or in business and commerce. In the previous chapter, the example of the Valero Energy acquisitions illustrates the importance of creating win-win situations for the employees of both parties to the merger. Transitions are rarely smooth in any given situation, but well informed employees will help solve the cross-cultural changeover problems.

- **Alienated customers** are often another byproduct of mergers and acquisitions. The Union Pacific-Southern Pacific Railroad merger and its resulting service disruptions and delays are classic examples of customer dissatisfaction following a merger. Expected improvements in products and services that do not materialize for whatever reason are major factors in alienating customers. Just as there is a corporate culture within a company, there is a customer culture among consumers. Sudden changes in goods or services brought about by mergers and acquisitions may not be viewed favorably by the end users.

Consider this hypothetical situation which, unfortunately, exemplifies the 83% of mergers that ended in failure over the last 20-plus years:

Wonder Widgets acquires Super Sprockets with the idea of improving cash flow and gaining greater market share. After the merger, however, the much touted synergy fails to materialize. Employee morale plummets. Because of the difference in the two corporate cultures, mass confusion sets in. Instead of managing strategically, managers are bogged down with daily, on the spot decision making as they put out the fires of poor coordination and miscommunication. Production slows, deliveries are delayed. The result is that previously happy customers become increasingly disenchanted. Many of those customers leave the merged company and look for competitors who are not in such organizational disarray. The damage to the merged company's brand is as bad as the actual lost revenue from the defecting customers. Worst of all, no one understood that it is easier-and far cheaper- to retain satisfied customers than to reclaim alienated ones.

- **Management spread too thin** is frequently another result of mergers. Some of the acquired company's management team will be laid off. That is the reality. A company can't have two sets of bosses. Often, however, valuable and needed managers from the acquired company leave the merged company because of real or imagined threats to their authority or to their jobs. This leaves the new company with too few managers, and leaves the remaining management team shorthanded, overworked, and spread too thin. Employees who now feel neglected by their overworked bosses get dispirited and think about leaving the company as well. What began as a "right-sizing" of managers and employees all too often turns into an avalanche of departing team members. Many times, the skilled and experienced people walk out the door along side the redundant people.

- **There are almost always losers** in merger situations. Some of those losses include jobs. If the acquired company was suffering from poor production in the first place, further reductions are predictable from the loss of staff. Efficiency, output, or both deteriorate, and the expected benefits of the merger vanish in puffs of destructive smoke. The intangible good will from customers is diminished. Finally, there are repercussions throughout the entire economy. The erosion of consumer confidence when huge layoffs are announced in major industries can have a ripple effect throughout the economy.

There are Good Mergers

It would be silly to propose the abolition of company mergers across the board. There are situations when mergers are beneficial to all parties concerned, but they are rarely inspired by lawyers and investment bankers. Nor do they create celebrity CEOs. In certain cases mergers can be a boon to both companies involved as well as the shareholders in those companies.

• Good mergers and acquisitions involve increasing market share. In mature industries where there are few new customers, mergers can be a way to gain customers and share without trying to pry the customers away from the competition. In younger markets where there are few established players, there is the possibility that a merger will enable the buyer to get bigger faster and become the predominant player before the competition can get established. When two small companies of the same industry or service merge in order to increase presence in the marketplace, the effect can be profitable to all concerned. Such mergers are never for the flash of media attention, but rather for the greater market coverage. In other words, the economy that can come with increasing scale. In these cases, the reasons for merger are not to improve weak cash flow or reverse declining market share. The desired result produces greater benefits to two companies which are already successful in a given market area.

• Good mergers happen when the companies involved in the transaction have similar cultures and business practices. This is likely the only situation when synergy actually makes any sense. The blending of the two companies is almost seamless without the loss of key personnel and the decline in overall employee morale.

- Good mergers are win situations for the employees. The resulting larger company may become more efficient and lower its costs with the result that it can increase salaries, benefits, or both for the workforce.

- Good mergers offer tangible benefits for the customers. Consumer satisfaction increases as a result of better service and/or better prices. Happy customers do not leave the company. This reduction in customer turnover can really improve profitability. It is cheaper to keep a current customer than it is to attract a new customer.

- Good mergers make good financial sense. The purpose of the merger is not to stroke the egos of the executive team. These mergers are based on sound business models that take the newly formed company forward in productivity and improved profitability. Profit rather than publicity is the purpose of the business after all.

> *"The message in <u>Making Companies Work</u> is that mergers and acquisitions rarely create value."*

Doing Away with the Mania

The current state of U. S. automakers is a clear example of the failure of mergers and acquisitions. While Japanese car manufacturers have, for the most part, concentrated on product improvement to increase sales and presence in the automotive marketplace, the major U.S. companies have concentrated on acquisitions that increased the size of their companies but did little to increase their value. In the first quarter of 2007, Toyota sold more cars than did General Motors and can now rightfully claim to be the largest auto manufacturer in the world. Increasing the size of a company through acquisitions usually only increases its complexity and has a negative effect on profits.

Simply doing away with mergers and acquisitions is not the answer since sometimes those arrangements are quite profitable. They are not, however, the primary purpose of business. If there is money to be invested (and there must be whenever a buyout is even considered) why does it not make sense to look first at how that revenue might best be channeled into the existing business? If the proposed buyer cannot get a higher return from investing in his own company, where is the logic that he can succeed by taking over another one?

To return to our hypothetical company, Wonder Widgets, its board of directors would be incredulous if the CEO suggested they start a new company publishing comic books. No one at Wonder Widgets knows the first thing about publishing and only the draftsmen can draw a straight line using a ruler. In a flash, the board would turn thumbs down on such a venture. Yet, if the CEO and some high powered investment bankers present to the board the possibility of buying out Korny Komics in order to increase the overall profitability of the company, the proposal is seriously considered! Merger mania strikes again.

Murphy's (Merger and Acquisition) Law

"Look at the figures, gentlemen. Our Wonder Widget Corp. revenues were $1 billion last year. Korny Komics nets a good half billion. If we buy them out, what could go wrong?"

What, indeed? Look at a few:
- The sales figures for Korny Komics represent a one-year snapshot of the company's business. It is more revealing to look at the last five years to determine the sales trend. Companies with robust sales prospects are usually not keen to sell. Why are they trying to sell in the first place?
- Expected cost savings do not materialize. In fact some of the costs actually go up. The costs incurred from combining two organizations are considerable.

- Key people at Korny Komics bail out when they realize that the management of Wonder Widgets will not understand the publishing business.
- There is a clash of business cultures between the merged entities. It may be as simple as the antipathy between manufacturing engineers in one company and creative types in the other company.
- Resources earmarked for business development in one of the companies are reallocated, usually to the acquiring company. After all, they are acquirers. Their projects are most important, aren't they?
- If this combining of companies was billed as a true merger, the biggest blow may come when it is time to determine which management will actually run the combined companies. Whenever there are winners and losers within a company, the company as a whole loses.

These situations happen routinely in the post-merger business world. You would think that companies would look askance at the buying of other companies. However, the current merger environment is as frenzied as ever. Clearly, there is something going on here besides good business practice. What is going on is what we call merger mania. In most cases the negatives of the mergers are far greater than the positives. In fact, it is difficult to see much benefit to anyone other than the principals involved: the CEOs, attorneys, consultants, and investment bankers. For the stockholders, the employees, and the customers these deals are losing propositions.

The message in Making Companies Work is that mergers and acquisitions rarely create value. Generally, the mergers serve to concentrate wealth from the many stockholders into the hands of a few principals. Growing a business-and on a macro level growing the economy-means selling more stuff to more customers. Stuff the customers want to buy. Stuff you already make, even if you have to keep making it better. It's what economists call organic growth. Growing from within by doing what you do best.

You may have heard the story about the acres of diamonds. There was a fellow who searched the world over for great wealth, only to discover that he had everything he needed in his own back yard. It's a good lesson for businesses. Instead of searching worldwide for other companies to acquire, concentrate on what you already do. Do it well; then do it better. Some call it playing to your strengths; others call it focusing on your core competencies. Either way, it involves delivering real value through your goods and services, and not creating paper value on a spreadsheet.

Keys to this Chapter

🔑 Mergers and acquisitions are almost always unsuccessful.

🔑 Shareholder wealth typically decreases after a merger.

🔑 Mergers and acquisitions are usually a sign of weakness within one or both companies.

🔑 Real business growth means selling more people more stuff.

Chapter Three

Fad of the Month Club

More than a few critics of American society have opined that we are a nation driven by fads. Collectively, Americans have a short attention span. What is "in" this year is "out" next year. Hair styles, clothing, music, even the colors of new cars all have their brief periods of popularity. The more chronologically experienced (read older) observers bemoan the loss of traditional ways and values.

Business executives are no different. The media likes to portray business people as stuffed-shirt, starched-collar, stiff, traditional, hide-bound, unyielding, and set-in-their-ways men (usually) in grey flannel suits who haven't had an original thought since the invention of the steam engine. The reality is that many business people are just as fad crazy as the rest of Americans. Despite their years of real world business experience-and often their formal business education-these normally steadfast executives are all too often willing to adopt the latest business fad, embrace the latest business guru, or institutionalize the bullet points from the latest business book.

One book, for example, centers on a rodent who can no longer find his usual food cache. The book has sold more than 3,000,000 copies. A more recent book-and another bestseller-tells the reader that once you have learned the secret knowledge contained within the book, you will never make another mistake because every decision you make will be the right one! We're sure every business man and woman in America will be glad to read that. No more MBA programs, no more financial analyses, no more educated guesses based on limited information. Just the illusory confidence that all your decisions will be correct. Shrinking market share? You were right. Negative cash flow? You go, gal. Company in bankruptcy? You're a business genius.

It's easy to understand why normally rational executives would chase business rainbows. After all, we are constantly reminded that the world is changing and that the rate of change is accelerating. Ya gotta keep up. And since everything else is changing, business has to keep changing to keep up. Sounds reasonable. So we look to the next business guru for THE NEXT BIG THING. We scan the latest business book, then pass it around to our colleagues so they can read it and "get" it. And we embrace each new management theory as the answer to whatever doesn't work in our organizations.

And how we love our buzzwords.

Let's Give it a Name

The CEO marches into the corporate boardroom and announces grandly, "We are implementing Best Practices into our management program and expect to see an improvement in our processes across the board." A reasonable person might be thinking, "Why haven't we been using our best practices all along?" Instead, this seemingly innovative idea sweeps across the business landscape. Senior managers get caught up much like college students at a pep rally. They've read the book, heard the guru, and brought in consultants to train everyone in this new discipline. This is "The Answer".

Boiled down to the basics, Best Practices is simply finding and utilizing the best ways to get things done. That, of course, is not a bad idea. What is bad, however, is giving it a name and clouding the issue with a bucket full of jargon that takes more time to learn than simply getting down to work. What often follows when the idea of Best Practices takes hold as some kind of magical elixir to management is an open floodgate of high sounding subdivisions such as Quality Control, Defect Tracking, Risk Management, and a myriad of other labels. All of this sounds good to the ear and looks great on a paper chart, but in most cases it is simply complicating the obvious. Instead of nomenclature, what is really needed is more elbow grease and common sense.

Another spinoff from Best Practices came to be known as Performance Engineering. This includes such arcane subdivisions as Rational Unified Process (RUP), non-functional requirements (NFR), System Volumetrics, and Unified Modeling Language sequence diagrams. Time spent learning the language is time that could have been better spent just running the business. Moreover, all this jargon tends to give the process the imprimatur of scientific validation. Performance Engineering, even once it is in place, will always be a matter of judgment calls. Between the system, the volume of work, and the actual users, Performance Engineering can never be reduced to scientific exactitude. Applying rationality to business processes can produce positive benefits. However, there is the danger, as there is with all other business fads, that Performance Engineering can divert management attention from the basics of running the business. The "how" overtakes the "why".

> *"... layoffs are always a failure of*
>
> *management."*

Shall We Dance?

The buzzword of Strategic Alliance made a big splash in the business world giving an impressive-sounding name to the simple idea of businesses working together to do things that would not be possible individually. Sometimes those alliances are intra-industry; other times inter-industry. The idea is good enough, but the reality often fails to produce a productive result. More than likely, an alliance of this sort is a halfhearted imitation of a merger or acquisition. The need for the alliance in the first place usually arises from a point of weakness—lack of development capital, access to larger markets, or the economics of scale. It also assumes that bigger is better. At least fifty percent of all such alliances fail. Usually, the reasons are incompatible business cultures and intra-alliance rivalry as the allies start to compete with each other.

Another fad in business is the Quality Circle which was introduced first in Japan. The idea is to have employees meet together and come up with changes they wish to present to management. Like many things cultural, the Quality Circle does not translate well into American business culture. What may be a positive cross communication in Japanese business is likely to turn into a company grievance session in American business. It has the potential of turning a tea party into a war zone. The perceived need for such an innovation reflects on the weakness of management to begin with. Henry Ford did not need a Quality Circle to make him realize the value of raising employee pay and benefits and reducing the work week. A CEO who comes down from his executive suite, walks the halls in his shirt sleeves, and talks personally to employees will understand the pulse of his organization in a superior way and be better able to effect appropriate change as needed.

A Rose is a Rose, and You're Still Fired

An outhouse with air freshener still stinks. Managers across the U.S. have been taught never to "fire" or "lay off" anyone. Instead, consultants teach them how to disemploy people with compassion.

This is supposed to preserve the dignity of the formerly employed as they stand in line at the Unemployment Office.

Here are some of the actual descriptors used by executives and their HR departments when they "dis-employ" their employees:

- ⊗ consolidation of operations
- ⊗ cost-containment measures
- ⊗ disemployment
- ⊗ downsizing the workforce
- ⊗ involuntary attrition
- ⊗ involuntary separation
- ⊗ outplacement
- ⊗ performance improvement plan
- ⊗ redeploying human assets
- ⊗ reduction in force
- ⊗ reengineering
- ⊗ restructuring
- ⊗ reverse hiring
- ⊗ rightsizing
- ⊗ smartsizing
- ⊗ streamlining operations
- ⊗ workforce reduction
- ⊗ termination
- ⊗ eternity leave

No matter the euphemism for individual firings and mass layoffs, the truth of the matter is that once the company decided it needed the employee, and now it doesn't. The reason for the firing could be overstaffing to begin with, unproductive use of labor, or a decline in business since the hiring. Regardless, layoffs are always a failure of management. Consider this: the business added employees as it grew to its present size. Suddenly, it seems, the company is overstaffed with previously necessary employees. Now there is a need to cut costs by reducing the company payroll. How did previously necessary employees become superfluous? The reason was management could not keep them busy. And that's because management could not keep growing the business. Of course there are business cycles to consider. But another way to Make Companies Work is to dispel the idea that employees are expendable. Most employees in corporate America are temp workers. They just don't realize it yet.

Layoffs are bad for the individuals, of course. But, they are just as bad for the companies involved. Layoffs are a sign of trouble. Layoffs are a sign that the business model is not working. And yet, executives are rewarded with bonuses and flattering magazine cover photos when they tacitly admit their failures by laying off their workers. There are countless examples of this kind of activity in the annals of American business. The US auto industry is a case in point. Massive layoffs at Ford came after the company bet the farm on trucks and SUVs even though there were clear indications that energy costs were an increasing worry for consumers. GMC and Daimler-Chrysler entered into mergers and acquisitions to increase revenues and unit sales, not to develop cars people actually wanted to buy and drive. What followed were the inevitable divestitures. Buying a company does not fix the problems in either the acquiring company or the acquired company. Meanwhile, Japanese auto makers in the US were busy producing fuel efficient and well-made cars- products that car buyers really wanted. The layoffs and the plant closures of the American auto makers are the price workers have had to pay for poor management.

The "New" Economy

Business fads come with their own trappings and nomenclature.

Suddenly in the last decade or so, everyone seems caught up with the idea that conventional wisdom is all wrong when it comes to the economy. So we had the information superhighway, new business paradigms, and the dawn of the new economy. Customers were unnecessary. Sales were irrelevant. It was all about first-mover advantage to grow big, fast. The hype was so pervasive that it was impossible to ignore. The new millenium and the new ecomony were upon us. And we believed, including corporate America. Especially corporate America.

Eventually, the hype led to companies each trying to be the next media and investor darling. Puffery and hyperbole gave way to creative accounting and financial fraud. Many people today long for the wonderful years of 1997-1999. Unemployment was low (although not much lower than today), profits were high, and we even had a federal budget surplus for the first time in forty years. Who could be blamed for thinking that the old rules of business and economics had become obsolete?

We now know that the last three years of the 20th century were too good to be true. Much of the reported data were bogus. Hundreds of companies reported profits that did not exist. The federal budget was balanced, in part, because of the corporate income taxes paid on these imaginary profits. It seems incredible that a company would voluntarily pay taxes on profit it did not make, but there was something much bigger going on. By reporting phony profits, companies could attract more capital. And more capital meant more growth. Remember "get big, fast"? More growth meant…higher prices for the company's stock. So here was the real business strategy, the real motivation. Do whatever it takes to pump up the price of your company's stock. Use the inflated stock value to buy other companies with real assets. Or cash in some stock to buy hard assets for the post-new economy: houses, boats, cars, and collectibles. That was the smart way to do business. The people who actually believed this stuff about the new economy were typically the employees of the dot-com companies. These employees turned out to be the real losers. Their stubborn belief in this new economy blather and their companies caused them to hold their stocks as the prices soared. But they also held on while the bubble burst. As a result, these dot-com millionaires-these true believers-came full circle from broke to rich to broke again. Many of the executives who understood what was going on and who gamed the system were eventually indicted and convicted. But, the rest got out and made out.

Also during the new economy years, moderation was tossed out the window as companies scrambled to get bigger and bigger. This idea only fed the merger and acquisition mania that more often than not ended in disaster. Office Depot CEO Mark Begelman admits he got caught up in the growth idea and acquired office supply companies that specialized in big-ticket sales to corporations. The net result was incredible headaches from not being able to handle the demands of the large companies. Buying a company is not at all the same as running a company. Over a period of three to four years after the acquisitions, revenues from large company orders only increased about six percent.

Many companies have grown to the point that they get noticed by investment bankers and others who insist that no growing company can survive unless it continues to grow and become a public company. Hard lessons have been learned from buying that idea. Companies have seen their stock prices fall and their financial backing fall away after making such a move. Lean operations and a strategy of internal growth are still sound business ideas.

Virtual business became another pie in the sky buzzword of the last ten years. The idea was to put a company's entire catalog on the internet and have independent sales people all over the company sell products by phone or from laptop computers. This selling model suffered from an almost void of corporate culture. There was no connection, no teamwork, and no camaraderie between employees. People in the field did not keep up with the new products, sometimes even selling discontinued items. There was no "virtual excitement" when a new product came online. As the virtual business model has developed, owners now realized that the business should be run from one central location where the interaction of people fans the excitement of making sales. The lesson here is that "virtual business" cannot be manned by "virtual people."

Another management fiasco presented itself as the fad of outsourcing began to catch on. As part of the "new" economy, the new buzzword was "outsourcing," which basically meant to allocate certain tasks to outside contractors, largely on the internet. Like the other fad ideas, it was quickly embraced as a means of cutting costs. But it was usually a case of leap before you look. One of the first areas targeted for outsourcing was the management and staffing of customer call centers. In other words, lay off your established, experienced, and loyal local employees. Instead, hire strangers nine time zones away to make your customers feel cared for. The major problem with outsourcing is more than time or language issues. The major problem is cultural, but not the way you would imagine. Here cultural refers to corporate culture. Outsourced customer service people simply do not have the personal dedication or the loyalty to your company that your own employees do. Your employees are-or should be- your biggest company cheerleaders. Properly motivated, your employees will represent your company with passion and sincerity. But, what we see far too often are companies who staff their customer service departments with the lowest paid, least skilled, and lowest status employees in the organization. Many companies are starting to rethink their outsourcing strategies. It is no longer a given that outsourcing produces a net positive return. Dollar costs may be reduced, but the diminution of customer satisfaction and the damage to the brand may well offset any dollar cost savings. In fact, there is a movement today to bring in formerly outsourced business functions because of the difficulty in managing and maintaining quality from a distance.

A word heard so frequently today that it almost grates on the nerves is "global economy" or "globalization." It really is nothing new. Commerce between countries has been around as long as there have been businesses. What it has come to mean of late, however, is breaking into foreign markets on their turf. Not a few companies have learned the expensive way that setting up shop in a foreign country is no slam dunk. In most countries the requirements include operating a joint venture with a local national holding the majority ownership. In many countries, the prospect of the government "nationalizing" a business is an ever present danger. The dreamy-eyed CEO who envisions tapping into a global market as a way to make his company grow had better do his homework.

First of all, there is the matter of building an entirely new infrastructure. Second, cultural considerations need to be considered. When Hang Ten marched into Thailand with the two little feet emblem on all their shirts, the Thais were shocked. Showing the bottom of the foot is an extreme insult in their culture. Globalization involves understanding other cultures and the business preferences involved. It calls for the reality check that all people around the world do not think about or have appreciation for all things American.

Consider all those state-of-the-art management systems that cost thousands of dollars for the software alone. Then, of course, new hardware and networking equipment are required. It is also typical that armies of consultants will be needed to install and customize the software. Finally, trainers are needed to show the employees how to change their procedures and processes so that the software works. Add it all up and that IT project will end up costing at least three times its original estimate. Incredibly, research has shown that half of all IT projects are never completed. They are just abandoned as the company gives up in frustration and moves on to the next big thing. Computerization has transformed our economy for the better. But the rush to computerize, the mania to upgrade, and the hype of integration have also become another type of business fad.

New systems are purchased and often obsolete by the time the installation is finished. To stay abreast, the company is convinced it needs more and more technology. Business starts to be run through emails and cell phones and voice mail. In a virtual world, employees no longer have to actually interact with the customers. What it often means is the elimination of any direct contact with the client. And the data reflect this. In many industries, customer satisfaction is low and getting lower. All the technology in the world cannot compensate for personalized customer service and communication.

Back in the late 1980s and the early 1990s, soothsayers were all predicting that fixed location corporations would largely disappear in the wake of virtual organizations. They predicted that by the turn of the century, most of the workforce would be working from home. They postulated that ecommerce would be the predominant mode of business. But they forgot a basic truth: computers don't buy or sell anything. People do business with people.

The Origins of Fads

Who dreams this stuff up, anyway? Here's one explanation. Some respected academicians in a highly regarded business school conduct research and publish a paper. The paper contains some good insights about effective management and might even coin some new terminology to reinforce those ideas. The ideas get exposure in the business press and sometimes in the popular media. Then some Business Guru adopts and adapts the information into a whole system that calls for reconstructing the way a company does business. Since many CEOs want to appear cutting-edge, they buy in. If the CEO is at all famous, other CEOs play business follow-the-leader and emulate the new management methods of the so-called thought leader CEO. "Under new management" has come to mean the same old managers using a new management theory. The new fad may not work and will probably be short-lived, but at least the directors, the employees, and hopefully the stockholders are impressed that senior management is in on the next big thing.

As the fad mushrooms and is further fanned by the media, consultants come out of the woodwork claiming to have used the new method for years with astonishing results. It is observable that these fads eventually lose favor only to be replaced by yet another new business model. Some of the fads may actually prove beneficial to the organization, but they are almost always a distraction from the principal business of business: selling stuff to customers that they want and/or need.

As this cycle repeats itself, it seems that the time between inception and abandonment grows shorter and shorter. In other words, fads seem to have life cycles just as products do. What makes these fads so destructive is that each purports to be The Answer. Each is the magic bullet, the panacea, the solution to all a company's ills. But the truth is that business success involves more than one theory, one buzzword, or one slogan. It takes a number of things to be successful in business. They are all really simple concepts, but the danger is that CEOs keep looking for that one-liner that will create higher profits, happier employees, and more satisfied customers.

I Know It When I See It

Supreme Court Justice Potter Stewart once said about obscenity, "I shall not attempt to define [it] . . . but, I know it when I see it." CEOs worth their salt can likewise spot a fad when they see one. Unfortunately, many of them do not look closely enough to recognize that some new management method is just another fad. If, in fact, they did look before they leapt, they might have taken note of the following:

- Fad systems usually claim to be beneficial to everyone, a sort of one-size-fits-all solution to business management.

Any rational person should immediately question that absurdity.

- Almost out of the blue, everyone is talking about this wonderful new method, especially in business conferences where consultants and industry experts are giving presentations that are, in reality, sales pitches for their services.

- The new method bears no resemblance to any time honored way of doing business. Of course not, it's new and innovative. This requires the company to tear down and rebuild systems already in place and working well.

- The proponents insist that the new system is simple but will be able to solve complex problems. You will, however, have to hire their consultants for proper implementation.

- Lofty but anecdotal claims about how the system has changed the fortunes of those who use it. Snake oil salesmen in the Old West had that tactic down pat.

- Nobody either can or will explain in simple English exactly how the system works. It is amazing that CEOs who do not understand a word of what is said about these fads seem to think that they are the elixir of life for an ailing company. The reasoning seems to be, "If I don't understand it, it must be revolutionary."

It's in Print, So it Must Be True

The old adage of not believing everything you hear and only half of what you see should be posted in every corporate boardroom. Unfortunately, that is rarely remembered as the media choose their next business superstar. One of the worst features of media attention is that cause and effect are often confused. Oversimplification and reasoning based on faulty or inadequate understanding are common in the popular press.

A classic example of media frenzy is the way Cisco Systems has been reported in the press. In the late 1990s, the company was hailed as the best example of an outstanding business where everyone was happy to go to work. By the year 2000, however, when the dot-com economy turned to the dot-bomb economy

Cisco was forced to lay off employees. The company that previously could do no wrong was now vilified in the press. The media assumption was that all the company's problems were created internally. Some problems may have been self-inflicted, but certainly not all. Cisco's core business was supplying network hardware. Within the space of 18 months, half of its market dried up as dot-coms closed their doors. This was a case of a well-run company with good products that had lost half of its market due to the collapse of the "new economy". It had sold real products to real customers for real dollars, but now the customers were gone. It took Cisco almost five years to recover, but by 2007 Cisco had climbed its way back and regained its dominant position in its market niche. If the company hadn't been managed so well, it would have become extinct along with many of its customers.

When reading about companies in the press, a heavy dose of skepticism is in order. The media has a tendency to oversimplify a story and to ascribe success or failure to one single aspect of a company's operation. Thus the media contribute to the propagation of business fads. When giving credit to some new fad management system for an outstanding success, the media overlook the day to day contributions of an entire workforce of dedicated employees. Market, economic, or political factors also are often not considered when the media decide to praise some company. Worse yet, some CEOs start to believe their own press coverage and start to overestimate their contribution to their companies' successes. This then becomes the basis for the celebrity CEO. When the company struggles, it's because of external factors. But when the company does well, it's the work of one person: the CEO and his management system du jour.

Resting on Laurels

There is a temptation in business (as in everything else) to rest on previous success. This is where the danger of believing one's own press comes into play. Suppose Tiger Woods had taken to heart the headlines that proclaimed him "the world's greatest golfer," and that he was "unbeatable." Believing the press coverage, he might never again bother with practice. He would now believe that he possessed the secret of golfing success. It sounds ridiculous, but that's how a lot of CEOs run their companies. What worked before, will work again, they reason. When the reality of changing conditions and markets proves otherwise, they grasp for that magic bullet that will make everything alright again. Tiger, on the other hand, continues to train, practice, and experiment, always looking for improvement. Even as he continues to win more tournaments than any other golf professional, Tiger Woods keeps in mind every week is a new tournament.

Business is the same principle. Not every good idea will work. There is no such thing as a perfect business strategy. Let's say that company XYZ demonstrates remarkable growth after initiating some new business process such as Six Sigma. That does not mean that every other company who uses that model will be equally as successful. There are many factors to consider and no two companies will be equipped to execute any business strategy in the exactly same way. If that were possible, all businesses would use the same formula with the same results and everyone would succeed. A trained monkey could figure that one out.

Survival in business requires real thinking, often very creative thinking. As many businesses in New Orleans simply folded after Hurricane Katrina, other entrepreneurs looked for ways to pick up the pieces. It was a natural disaster and not bad management that caused the situation. One business was a brand spanking new cooking school that had started out with a splash after the owner, Aaron Wolfson, sank everything he owned or could borrow into the venture. Then, in an instant, a city of over a half-million population was suddenly home to fewer than 200,000 people. In the aftermath of Katrina, no one was interested in taking cooking classes.

Surveying the situation, Wolfson saw that the grocery stores were short on food items and less than half of the city's legendary restaurants were back in operation. Instead of waiting around for government grant money and a return of the populace, Wolfson had an epiphany. The Savvy Gourmet Cooking School quickly restyled itself as a restaurant utilizing the advantages of not having been damaged in the flooding, still able to run its air conditioning and show television, and being able to provide wireless internet service. Within three days after reopening, he had all the customers he could handle.

Another New Orleans business that had been involved in coastal restoration saw that it needed to offer completely different services to the storm ravaged area. New Line Environmental moved into construction and even started a new venture called the Hurricane Guy, Inc. They created revenue by offering to board up houses, clean out refrigerators, and provide other such services that were desperately needed in the city at the time.

The point is that pure chance plays a great role in the success or failure of a business. But what is important is the company's response to the situation. Disasters in business need not be limited to natural phenomena, either. Great upheavals in the business world also occur with political and economic changes. Companies like Cisco don't just react; they respond by following the basic rule of business. Find out what else your customers need, and then see that they get it.

Business Buzz Words

Business management fads usually come in packages labeled with catchy acronyms or phrases, business speak for the mouthful of words that name the latest craze. In many cases, they are associated with IT (information technology). The benefits to business of computerization are wonderful indeed, but remember that Henry Ford, Thomas A. Edison, and Alfred Sloan were able to build business empires without laptops and email.

Consider the following processes and methodologies. None is bad. Each has its applications. But, none is the answer for a struggling company. They are merely tools to help businesses run better. Beware the consultant who tells you (and sells you) that any of these is The Answer.

TQM actually began in the 1950s before the advent of big business computer systems. The acronym stands for Total Quality Management, a label that should appeal to anyone in business. The general idea behind TQM is to bring together all aspects of running a company with the goal of customer satisfaction. Such an obvious business aim is hardly a burning bush. Anyone in business with a modicum of intelligence can see the value of creating satisfied customers.

By the 1980s, the idea of TQM caught on again in American business. The hype was "do it right the first time and eliminate waste." Gradually, like a mutating virus, TQM strands began to develop from the common origins of the idea. With greater technology at hand, these approaches became more and more complicated with chapters and sub-chapters of implementation.

The idea of TQM is that the business is viewed as a total organism that includes management in every division and every employee of each division. Practically, it suggests that everyone in the business is an important cog in the overall wheel, and suggestions for improved efficiency may come from any level. The laudable aim of TQM is to produce products or services that satisfy the expectations of the buying public. There is nothing wrong with such an objective.

What eventually occurs, however, when TQM becomes the corporate law of the land is that a morass of complicated analyses and changes are introduced and even institutionalized. As the relationship between senior management and employees evolved, so did processes and procedures within the companies. TQM began focusing on minutia which led to endless meetings and organizational changes. Whole systems were set up to initiate improvements. Complicated formulas were devised to coordinate demand and production.

Employee empowerments were structured under TQM which gave ownership to line management, nominally at least. The jumble eventually produced quagmires of planning sessions, pressures to increase development times, challenges to previous goals and yardsticks for meeting new targets. Its aim was to involve every aspect of a business, every employee, and every department into a unified organization.

As a business idea, TQM is a praiseworthy goal. By transforming a business so that everything is done right the first time and waste is eliminated, clearly higher standards are met and more customers are satisfied. Nevertheless, as a silver bullet, TQM tends to become unwieldy and unnecessarily complicated. It further rests on a faulty assumption that eventually all mistakes can be avoided. However, TQM contains a catch 22 that encourages early detection of problems and halting of production to prevent further mistakes from being shipped out. Sounds good until you realize that production can plummet even though quality is increasing.

Modern TQM opens other cans of alphabet soup such as SPC (statistical process control) which produces charts and numbers to monitor production. Somebody has to gather the data and make the charts. Further complicating the process are Failure Mode and Effects Analysis (FMEA) which is supposed to serve as a preventative measure. TOPS (Team Oriented Problem Solving) is designed to increase teamwork while actually solving business problems. Subsequently, the TQM team puts focus on CONQ (Cost of Non-Quality). These are but a few of the offshoot areas that fall under the umbrella of TQM, but they might raise the question as to when actual work gets done with all the time spent on not-so-silver bullet projects. The danger here is that the focus is on the process instead of the customer. An organization can get so engrossed in doing things right that it forgets to do the right things.

There is no question that the quality of goods or services should be top priority. The question here is, "Just how complicated does the process of delivering quality have to be?"

Although these management practices all share characteristics of business fads, they each have their positive aspects. Total Quality Management (**TQM**) is praiseworthy just for its name alone. Any CEO who does not aim for total quality in his or her management style is falling short of the job. The concept, however, lacks a healthy dose of reality. It should not take hours and hours of company time to organize and train for the obvious. That is, any well-run company should be looking to avoid mistakes. It does not take numerous committees and endless meetings to get that across. Any company planning to stay in business which discovers a problem must decide whether to continue turning out more of the mistakes based on the rarity of the defects versus the cost of shutting down production. Making TQM the centerpiece of your organization is missing the big picture. Processes are tools, methods of serving and satisfying customers. The big danger here is that companies and their managers get so wrapped up in these faddish methods that they lose sight of the basic truth that people sell products to other people who buy them. You develop a relationship. You don't manage it. And customer satisfaction in all areas should be the goal, not quality to the neglect of production, delivery times, or profit.

ERP (Enterprise Resource Planning) enters the picture when it is touted as the end-all for a unified production system because all company data, regardless of system modules, is stored in one centralized database. Actually, to qualify as an ERP program, the software has only to combine two formerly independent systems into one package. Thus, a program that combines accounting and payroll would be considered an ERP system. More advanced examples of ERP might draw together in one software application such things as manufacturing, raw material supply, management of storage, human resources available and needed, as well as other related aspects of a business.

ERP incorporates both front office and back office into a centralized database. Although there are software packages available to help smaller companies set up ERP to coordinate formerly independent systems within the organization, larger companies usually employ their own IT specialists. Problems may arise like being unable to pay a bill or salary for the lack of a proper code number.

All Under One Roof

Proponents of **ERP** had the idea that everything would be smooth, business would run better, and customers would benefit if all aspects of a company where kept in one database. Here come the more expensive computer systems, the customized software, and the high priced consultants. The idea might be really good for certain manufacturing operations or even for international retail outlets. The human tendency of safeguarding departmental autonomy can be overcome in some instances. In other operations, ERP might be likened to a family bank account set up because Aunt Martha always overdraws her individual account. Setting up an account so that every member of the family draws from the same pool of money is not going to change Aunt Martha's bad habits. She is still going to hide her transactions until someone sits down to balance the account. Imagine the same sort of resistance in a large company when Research and Development refuses to forward its data to the central location for fear that Sales and distribution will know too much about R&D business.

When trying to implement a program such as ERP, it often develops that newer, bigger, and more expensive computer hardware and software are required. This further complicates matters because of the amount of lost time getting the new system set up and online for all departments concerned. The related software programs come in plain vanilla versions which, while cheaper to buy initially, may call for expensive tweaks to customize. This actually works against the idea of best practices in a given industry.

> **"A number of surveys conducted between 1995 and 2001 concluded that 50% of IT projects had been failures."**

A close look at many fad solutions often reveals that those solutions are more complicated and costly than the original perceived problem. In almost every case where ERP is introduced, a great deal of customization is required where company work practices do not fall within the default configuration of the basic system. The choice then becomes: spend millions to customize a standardized program or change your work processes and accounting systems to conform to the programmers' ideas of how business should be run. But extensive customization of software defeats the purpose of buying off-the-shelf programs. And the greater the degree of customization, the longer it will take to install, debug, and train, not to mention discard when the final product still doesn't work properly. Furthermore, customization often fails for the simple reason that the programmers are not business people. They do not know your company and may have only casual knowledge of your industry.

Other problems arising out of adopting an ERP software program include having employees who never understand its use, employee turnover that requires constant technical training on an arcane program, license renewal fees that drives up the total cost of ownership, and the blurring of accountability for project failure because so many departments and people are involved in the implementation. Any weak link in the implementation can and will cause a breakdown in the system. The human foible of wanting to safe-guard territory may lead to non-sharing of important data. Computer security also becomes a major concern. While ERP may be beneficial on a scale appropriate to some businesses, clearly this is not a uniform solution to good business across the board.

Six Sigma has been touted by some as the heir apparent to TQM, though in net benefit it appears to offer little advantage. This model assigns roles to various management leaders within the organization to bring about a new level of competition that may be more destructive than beneficial. Six Sigma has a hierarchy of managers ranging from Executive Champions down to Black Belts and on to Green Belts, labels borrowed from the world of martial arts. CEO Jack Welch of GE reportedly told his managers that if they wanted to get promoted they "had better be Black Belts."

Training under Six Sigma is quite rigorous and is oriented toward statistics, project management plans, and solving problems. The cost of the training, typically from $15,000 to $25,000 for a Black Belt, is expected to be offset by savings. The personnel designated as Master Black Belts and Black Belts are the team members who work exclusively on Six Sigma projects.

The main idea behind Six Sigma is to eliminate virtually all types of errors and waste in production that result in duplicated work. CEOs who have pushed Six Sigma claim billions of dollars saved for their companies. The central focus is to reduce defects in process and products in order to reduce waste, lower costs, and create higher customer satisfaction through higher quality products.

One of the major problem considerations involves training managers who can read and understand the statistics generated by the program. Since it is basically a statistical method, even the production employees need to have an understanding about statistics. And yet more and more young people are becoming math phobic. States have had to mandate specific math courses and skills to get high schoolers to take algebra and geometry. Very few high school students ever take a statistics course. So Six Sigma requires a level of understanding that most employees have no background for.

Six Sigma sounds impressive. It also sounds like a military operation. While its goal may be to achieve a quality of flawless perfection, it is nonetheless an approach compelled by data. The idea is to streamline everything from supply to manufacture to distribution and all points in between. It is claimed that literally thousands of companies have jumped on the Six Sigma bandwagon. The question remains, though, what does it all mean to the customer?

The point to be considered here is how all these fad programs are focused. In most cases-and Six Sigma is no exception-the focus is internal rather than external. It may eventually improve the flow of work within an organization, but what does it mean to the customer? While it is true that some company CEOs have claimed savings of over a quarter of a million dollars per project by using Six Sigma, how does that translate into customer satisfaction and increased sales?

Finally, with complicated programs such as Six Sigma, how much of the original idea in the data gathering process eventually gets thrown out? Can customer relationships really be reduced to statistics in a sheaf of papers? It is arguable that Six Sigma is just a jazzed up version of TQM, but a version with a higher price tag.

Six Sigma originated with Motorola and quickly spread to other major U. S. companies. Notable among those companies are

General Electric, Ford, Amazon.com, the Boeing Company, and Bank of America. Although based on sound mathematics, it is another management model that has been seen as The Answer. As a quality control methodology, it is a useful tool. But it is not the way to run a business. Just ask Motorola how much Six Sigma has helped it lately. Motorola was the leader in analogue cell phones for a while. High quality cell phones manufactured, no doubt, within a Six Sigma environment. But Motorola was late recognizing the industry transition to digital telephony. So the company became masterful in manufacturing obsolete phones. Here we have another case of doing things right instead of doing the right things. The recent lack of buzz over Six Sigma would suggest that this useful tool has the elements of a fad. And as a fad, it has the risk of distracting companies from their true purpose of determining customer's wants and needs and then satisfying those same desires.

Reengineering became a corporate buzzword after a series of books were published by Michael Hammer and James A. Champy. The concept was that of a radical redesign of business processes and procedures. It introduced the idea of cross-functional teams that eliminate the time wasted in passing tasks from one department or division to another.

In effect, Henry Ford practiced reengineering when he transformed Ford Motor Company into production line manufacturing thus radically changing the production ideas among his employees. The management buzz over reengineering reached its peak in the mid 1990s, becoming just another of the fashionable silver bullet trend ideas to fall out of favor.

Reengineering is a buzzword that lingers long after it came and went as the management fad of its day. In simple terms, reengineering advocates a complete overhaul of a company that is not performing up to expectations. There certainly are and always will be companies which have started the downward slide that might be saved by examining and correcting weaknesses. The idea behind reengineering is in some ways like reinventing the wheel. We do not tear down the house to upgrade the air conditioning system, though there will be inconveniences and certain modifications that must be done in the process.

It might be safely assumed that an existing company has done something right in its history or it would not have managed to come as far as it has. To paraphrase and old country saying, "If it ain't broke, don't fix it." In reengineering a company, the need is to discover exactly what is not working and fix that. The fad of reengineering, however, tends to completely rework the entire company rather than focus on the root causes of the problems. Reengineering zeal can lead to change for the sake of change. Burn the place down (metaphorically speaking) so we can rebuild it from the ground up.

Revisiting Chapter 2, it is clear that many companies solve reengineering problems by selling the company. The buying company is expected to come in with the new broom to sweep clean. In effect, the idea is to let someone else be the heavy, doing the layoffs and making all the needed changes. History shows, though, that those acquisitions seldom work.

CRM (Customer Relationship Management) is another IT darling that focuses on the consumer by capturing and analyzing customer data. Such analyses may focus on a very broad range of purposes and ultimately involve both sales or service representatives or direct communication that does not involve those people. It almost has an Orwellian tinge to it—capturing information from individual customers, assigning that data to a centralized database, and utilizing the information to formulate company strategies. The CRM paradigm seems to be the latest rage for success in business.

Collaborative CRM is the new wave of self-service interaction that may take many forms such as the internet, email, or the increasingly utilized interactive voice response (IVR) telephone systems. All of this is supposed to capture consumer response in an efficient, time saving way. It's highly doubtful that having your customer communicate with your server to update your database will actually create an intimate customer relationship.

CRM software requires data input from almost every department in a company. This usually requires the company to change all of its software so that all departments can share data. Of course, this requires better computers, more servers, even mainframes. Sound familiar? The purpose is to know everything knowable about the customers. Therefore, the better CRM systems are highly intrusive. But even the most powerful system can't know a customers mind. The best ones are still only rough approximations of the tastes and preferences of the customers. Most marketing managers will privately admit that they have no idea how their CRM implementations work, if the data are useful, or whether there is an ROI on the time and expense of the stalling the system.

A greater criticism of CRM is the name and the philosophy behind the name. It is more than a little presumptious-and quite a bit arrogant-to think that a company can "manage" a customer relationship. To manage is to control, to compel a person, a process, or a machine to conform to established standards. You don't manage relationships, especially the relationship between two equals. So the conceit in CRM is that if we know enough about the customer-if we have enough data on him-we can get him to buy more of our stuff. This leads us to the biggest criticism of all: CRM treats the customer as though he were one big wallet. CRM analyzes previous buying behavior to see what else we can sell him.

True customer service involves satisfying the customer through every interaction with him. Customer satisfaction involves far more than the actual purchase transaction. It includes service before the sale, after the sale, and offering the products best suited for the customer's needs. Sometimes, it involves convenient buying, financing, and delivery. And at all times, customer service should be focused on the total customer experience and not on products yet to be purchased.

First-mover advantage is another of the popular concepts that has businesses scrambling to be the "first kid on the block." The idea is that the company that introduces a product or service first has the advantage of gaining large market share before competitors can jump on the bandwagon. One of the advantages of first-mover programs is being able to preempt resources such as prime retail locations. Early profits from first-movers can be quickly reinvested to the benefit of the company. Sometimes the products of the first-mover actually become the popular name of an entire category of similar products that follow (e.g., Kleenex is often used by the general public for any tissue).

The idea of First Mover is nothing novel. A First Mover company obviously has a 100% market share when a new product or service is introduced. It is not a guarantee of dominance in the marketplace, however. History is filled with examples of someone introducing something new only to be out distanced later by those who came along with similar but improved products and services.

The lesson that should be learned from first movers is that constant change and improvement is the only way to retain the First Mover advantage. Being first to market is less important to the vast majority of consumers than being best to market. Only 1-5% of a given market consists of pioneers-buyers who love innovation so much that they have to be first on their block to have a new product. By the time you have reached the early adopters and the mainstream buyers, your competitors have released their copycat products. And those products probably have features you overlooked.

Recent failures in the dot-com and tech sectors have shown that, for the most part, first mover advantage is a myth. The company that is first to market is a pioneer. Market acceptance can never be known in advance. Costs cannot be quantified since the technology is new and the economies of scale are as yet unknown. Time after time, a first-mover company has entered a market only to discover that the customers wanted something a little different, a little more suitable to their needs. Any advantage from being a first mover is almost always negated by the fact that the first-mover is really doing market research for the rest of the industry. The company that is second to market-even third- has the advantage of observing this test marketing. The second-mover can then introduce the "new and improved" version that has all the features lacking in the first-movers model. Golfers use this concept all the time. Golfers love it when they get to putt after another player whose ball was between theirs and the cup. These second-putters get to watch the track of the first ball and observe how that ball rolls toward the cup. You don't hear so much about first-mover advantage anymore. Today, many companies are willing to let someone else be the market guinea pigs. They then can enter the market with products the customers really wanted. Less market research, less market risk, and shorter learning curves.

No Bullet in Sight

To be sure, problem solving is an important aspect of making companies work. The Ford Motor Company's 8 D's define the need of an overall system of quality initiative by developing a program that involves a teamwork approach. The D's represent 8 disciplines necessary to make the program work. Specifically, this approach works best on solving problems that come up continually, recurring year after year. Yet utilizing the 8 D's at Ford has not proven to be a magic bullet for revving up an underperforming automaker. The fact is that there is nothing new, nothing beyond mere common sense in most of the slickly polished gimmicks for internal improvement of a company.

Every company must have a strategy for doing business and staying in business. That simple fact should be obvious. Business strategy is all about making the company distinctive from other companies in the same or similar business. Acquisitions and outsourcing have nothing to do with becoming the preferred vendor for your customers. They do not offer a unique selling proposition. Doing things simply to look stylish or even cutting-edge is not sound business strategy.

Strategy should produce growth, but growth in and of itself is not the ultimate goal. It is possible to grow a company into failure. The Gap may be a good example of how that can happen. Starting with a unique product line that appealed to a specific market segment, The Gap expanded quickly and diversified to appeal to different age groups. Growth was the mantra. Bigger was better. Much of the motivation for rapid growth was to gain favor with stock analysts who would recommend the stock to investors who, in turn, would bid up the price of the stock. Higher stock prices meant the company could attract more capital to do what? Grow the company even more. For several years the company had grown by appealing to a distinct niche. But then, it was growth for growth's sake-growth to satisfy Wall Street. Along the way, the growth began to dilute the brand. New stores took time and resources from existing stores, and their existing customers. Sales figures began to plateau. No money was put back into redecorating and revitalizing Gap and Old Navy stores. In early

2007, The Gap listed itself with Goldman Sachs, looking for a buyer. Somewhere in the midst of its phenomenal growth, company strategy that had once made the stores unique went missing.

Follow the Leader

Business fads, by definition, cause companies to become copycats of other companies, even though their situations may be entirely different. The common sense knowledge that what works for one company is not necessarily a formula for all gets tossed aside. For example, XYZ Corp. gets a sales boost after implementing CRM. Therefore, the thinking goes, if we all adopt CRM, we'll be successful. Never mind that correlation does not mean causality. It could have been coincidence. We can't be sure that CRM caused the sales increase. It could have been-and usually is-something else. But instead of looking for that something else, it's so easy to jump on the CRM bandwagon as companies look for the easy fix.

Nurturing a customer relationship is, or should be, the foundation for any business. Without the customer, there is no business. Every kid who has ever set up a lemonade stand knows that. Kids also understand that their curbside enterprise does not need the elaborate operational models of Coca Cola, Inc. Nevertheless, CEOs will fall all over themselves in a rush to put in place the latest fad in management systems. It begins to appear that many CEOs, lacking ideas of their own, start grasping at any "new thing" that makes them look like they know what they are doing. Maybe a new thing can make them a celebrity CEO.

Do We Really Need a Cult?

Admittedly, there are good and workable ideas in the alphabet soup of modern management methods. Some of those have actually improved companies dramatically. However, the cult-like nature of these systems that begins to draw desperate followers is disturbing. They tend to draw single-minded adherents and practitioners looking for The Answer-the one big idea that will make everything right. As the fads gain traction, we see the rise to prominence of a "chosen few" consultants who are keepers of the knowledge and who will set up the magic management system. These various systems come with their specific rules and elaborate certifications. If a few years pass and the expected results never materialize, no matter. Everyone has forgotten how the whole thing started anyway. And besides, we have this neat new program that is going to solve all our problems.

The IT Factor

Some of you may remember the "IT" girl. She had that certain something-she had "it". Today, companies have "it" as well. Only the IT stands for Information Technology. And woe to the company that doesn't have "IT". If you want to have "IT", if you want to boast of your ERP and CRM, then you'll need to invest in upgraded computer hardware and software, not to mention the charges for customizing the software, training, and data entry/conversion.

Perhaps one reason so many companies have seen IT systems as a management tool is because IT itself is touted as the thing that will solve your problems. From our air traffic control system to the IRS computer upgrades, everything will be swell if only we have the latest and greatest IT. Somehow it is overlooked that "the latest thing" is a euphemism for "fad." Better to have last year's IT up and running than buy "state-of-the-art" equipment that never works properly and is now sitting in boxes in the storeroom. There is a tendency to jump into some of these high sounding management programs because they are fashionable. Unfortunately, they are also expensive failures in many cases.

A number of surveys conducted between 1995 and 2001 concluded that 50% of IT projects had been failures. Sometimes, the project never did what it was supposed to do. Other times, the project was so problematic it was abandoned. In other words, the chances are that an IT initiative is as likely to fail as it is to succeed. It's like the old joke that "to err is human but to really foul things up you need a computer." And when the projects do meet some measure of success, costs of 200-300% over the estimates are not uncommon. Thus, many IT projects waste time, money, and resources. Worst of all, they distract management from its mission of serving customers.

Transforming a company does not need to involve a lot of new equipment, high powered computer systems, or lengthy empowerment seminars. Needed changes do not have to cost a great deal of money. Some changes and upgrades do involve considerable investment. But the lesson here is that cost does not equal quality, and complexity does not ensure success.

A Trip Through the (IT) Graveyard

- In 2004, it is has been reported that Ford Motor Company abandoned a newly deployed purchasing system after wasting $400 million on its development.

- In 1999, Hershey Foods Co. installed a new ERP program that ended up causing a loss of over $150 million.

- 1997 in the State of Washington, a new IT system for DMV (Department of Motor Vehicles) was cancelled after $40 million had been spent.

- That same year, the IRS blew $4 billion on a new tax modernization effort. The Service never could get the system running and decided to abandon the entire project.

- In 1994, the State of California had spent $44 million before canceling a new DMV system.

Avis Europe PLC, Nike, McDonalds, CIGNA, K-Mart, United Way, and Allstate Insurance are just a few of the major companies and entities that have cancelled expensive IT management projects because of system failures, cost overruns, and/or loss of revenue after the projects were installed. Information on these and other IT disasters is readily available on the internet, in business magazines, and journals. Why do CEOs not do a little bit of that kind of research before selling their boards on reinventing the wheel? The most common scenarios when expensive IT management programs are attempted are well documented. The cost of the new software is often trebled by the time new hardware is installed. The charges for the analysts and programmers make for additional cost overruns. The new system does not interface with what is already in place. Companies often find that they have to change methods and ways of conducting business to fit the new program rather than have the program fit the company.

Leadership and Culture

Generally speaking, changes in a company amount to real changes in the company leadership. In many cases the priority should not be to restructure the company, but rather to improve the leadership. Before a CEO goes shopping for a magic bullet, he or she should take stock of the way the company is being led at the moment. Identify the weaknesses in the leadership and many other problems will take care of themselves.

Second, a good look at corporate culture may result in subtle changes that have an effect on company performance. Corporate culture entails relationships within the company, for sure. More importantly, it is about the relationship of the company to customers. There are some notable examples of companies that have turned their fortunes around by placing more emphasis on customer satisfaction. We will look closely at some of these in the final chapter.

CEOs and their boards also would do well to heed the lessons from history to avoid making the mistakes of others. Henry Ford is a prime example of a man whose leadership worked, though not without some failures along the way. Few remember that it was Henry Ford who raised the daily pay for the best workers from $2.35 to $5.00. He was criticized by his peers for establishing an 8-hour work day and a 5 day work week-standards which later became commonplace. The effect of these measures was to have fewer turnovers and therefore less time spent training new people. It established a corporate loyalty that helped make Ford leapfrog the 200 other car manufacturers to become the largest car company in the world.

On the other hand, Henry Ford made some blunders. Foremost was his refusal for many years to upgrade the Model T or to offer it in different colors. To his later regret, Mr. Ford once declared that the customer could have any color car he wanted as long as it was black. These decisions saw Ford's sales plummet in the mid-1920s as competitors began offering product upgrades, model changes, and perhaps most important, different paint colors. In 1926, Henry Ford finally agreed to start producing a new model, and the Model A Ford came into production. Over 4 million were sold during the next 4 years. After the success of the Model A, the company started introducing model changes annually, a practice that is used by the entire industry today.

Nevertheless, by the mid-1930's the price of a Ford had dropped from $600 to $350, and Ford's market share continued to decline. Where Ford once owned the car market, it became number 2 behind the upstart company known as General Motors.

The early, phenomenal success of Henry Ford can be attributed to his making needed changes within his organization to speed production and cut costs. His company became the ultimate vertically integrated company. By 1929, Henry Ford had successful dealerships on six continents. And all without a single IT system or business acronym.

Leaner, Meaner, and More Productive

As admirable as it may seem to trim the fat out of production and aspire to near perfection, it all means nothing if the customers do not want what the company produces, or worse yet, do not want to buy anything from the company. Today, some big box companies like Wal-Mart have long understood that truth and others, like Home Depot, are learning it the hard way. When Home Depot opened up a blog for customers (or former customers) to air their grievances, the company CEO had to apologize publicly and promise to correct the problems. The fight now is to win back customers—a feat much harder than keeping them in the first place.

Keys to this Chapter

Fads are fun. We are drawn to them because they are new and promise to be The Answer.

Fads become a problem when the entire organization is made over to follow the new management theory. Business is still based on making a profit by satisfying customers' needs and wants.

There never was a new economy. It was based on hype and fraud as millions of people can now attest.

CRM is no substitute for interpersonal relationships.

IT infrastructure is just a tool to help you achieve your true business purpose. Don't let IT capability and complexity distract you from serving your customers.

First Movers are generally first failures. Let someone else be the test market.

Chapter Four

Eyes on the (Wrong) Prize

Many business owners and executives show real passion and enthusiasm in their jobs. Unfortunately, their passion is misdirected. Celebrity CEOs focus on themselves and their personal gain. Fad driven executives devote their enthusiasm to the big idea that will put their companies over the top. And empire building CEOs fixate on sales growth. Each of these executives gets encouragement and support from directors, stockholders, and sometimes analysts who buy the company story. In case after case few people ask the simple question, "but are you making any money"?

The purpose of business is to make a profit by supplying customers with goods and services that they want. There are only two elements in that proposition: profit and satisfied customers. CEOs and boards of directors continually use and misuse other standards for success to the detriment of the employees, the stockholders, and the customers. Pleasing customers and producing perennial profits are not exciting or heroic. Seeing your CEOs photo on the cover of Fortune magazine is exciting. Reengineering your supply chain for JIT so that your TQM initiative supports your Six Sigma program while your IT infrastructure hardening allows your ERP to incorporate ERM: now that's sexy! Customers are just a rectangle on a flow chart. Profit is just a paper construct under the accrual accounting system. Bigger company, more sales. That's how you get promotions and raises.

Perhaps it's not so surprising then why everything seems to be emphasized except profit and customer service. Look at the incentives. If your department grows you get a promotion and a raise. If your company grows, your CEO gets a bonus and a raise. Rarely is there any question of, "but did you make any money"? This is why you see the great disconnect between executive pay and executive performance. Everyone's eyes are on the wrong prize. Profits up? CEO gets a raise and a bonus. Profits down? CEO gets a raise and a bonus. It has gotten so crazy that when struggling companies get taken over their CEOs get bonuses for presiding over failing companies. Even bankruptcy is now seen as successful management. It is common for bankrupt companies-Chapter 11 reorganizations and Chapter 7 liquidations-to pay their executive teams bonuses for essentially running their companies into the ground. Worse, the employees are getting their hours reduced, their wages reduced, or getting laid off (taking eternity leave) because of the companies' financial problems. Has it occurred to any of these CEOs that the reason their companies are in trouble is because of their focus on sales, fads, executive nest feathering? Faddism and ill-fated mergers and acquisitions have pushed aside sound business practices because of the mistaken idea that these things are the prize, the wizard's wand that will enrich a company's position in the market. Even the idea of "market share" that is so frequently bandied around in business meetings is not necessarily the answer to greater profits. A company can increase its market share and still go broke. Still, management continues to look in wrong directions for what is often right under their noses.

Why More Sales are Not the Prize

More sales do not translate into greater profits. If sales are increasing but the profit margin is decreasing, there comes a point where additional sales will cost you money. Many times, selling additional product means lowering the price to less than your costs. That's a warning sign that the company's products have saturated or bored the market. Another warning sign is the increase in cash reserves. On the surface, having a lot of cash makes a company look financially solid. But more often than not, it is a warning sign. Large cash reserves mean that the company cannot find any good places to use the money. All that cash is an implicit recognition that the return on additional product sales is poor. Why sell more stuff if you are going to lose money on each sale? All that cash is also an admission that management does not have the vision or the strategy to determine what customers want now. Cash is a function of the production and selling cycles. Cash reserves not needed for operations should be reinvested to create more profit or paid out to the owners-stockholders. We read about companies every day that have more than a billion dollars in cash reserves while the companies themselves are actually in danger of failing.

Increasing sales (or market share, if one prefers that measurement) may come at a cost that actually lowers or eliminates a company's profit margin. There are costs and other limitations involved that must be taken into consideration.

- Will greater sales put a strain on the company's ability to produce the products?
- Will a much greater and more expensive advertising budget be required?
- Will price cuts be needed to encroach into competitors' shares of the market?
- Will any growth in sales result in stepped up competition from larger competitors?
- Are all customers—especially the new ones—actually profitable?

While no one would question the necessity of robust sales in any business, it should also be crystal clear that sales are not the end-all of profitable commerce.

Many home-based or virtual companies have learned this lesson the hard way. By quickly recruiting sales associates throughout the country, complications arose that were the direct result of the push for a rapid growth in sales activity. One virtual company tells of the simultaneous hiring of agents across the country and the problems that subsequently arose from a sales volume that the company was not equipped to handle:

- It was impossible to train all the salespeople so quickly.
- It was difficult to keep salespeople up to date on current product offerings.
- Lack of training and product knowledge resulted in dissatisfied customers and loss of repeat orders.

Eventually that company saved itself in the nick of time by returning everything to a central location where everyone was working out of the same office. All sales handled out of the central office were up to date. The sales staff was current on both products and prices. The volume of sales did not increase, but the profit margins did. Complaints were reduced to almost nil as orders stayed within the small company's ability to generate products in a timely manner.

The same phenomenon occurs when an already centralized company launches a new promotion or cuts prices to boost sales and increase market share. Profits can evaporate because costs exceed prices. But just as important, sales can suffer when the organization is under prepared and ill equipped to handle the increase in sales volume.

The importance of sales to any business cannot be understated, but it is never a matter of sales alone. Businesses must be looked at holistically. If a company produces a large number of products but no one is out there selling them, the result is obvious. However, using sales alone as an indicator of business success is actually a throwback to the emergence of the industrial age. When Henry Ford introduced the idea of assembly-line mass production, his idea was to produce a car that was so affordable that every family in the USA could own one. To be sure, Ford sold an incredible amount of automobiles. By limiting thinking in that manner, sales eventually dropped drastically low because of Ford's tunnel vision about the market. Ford's idea of selling cheap cars to the nation began to fail because product changes that added value to the customer were not even considered. The eyes had been on the wrong prize.

Mass Customization Seemed like a Good Idea. . .

It sounded like the definitive answer to business growth—work directly with the customer and produce products individualized to that customer. It started off with a bang when the principles of assembly line productivity were coupled with individual customer requirements. Today the picture is not so rosy. Because of globalization, competitors can enter the market by producing the same products at a lower cost. This has become especially true as China and India entered the IT age. In textiles, the foreign producers have all but obliterated American manufacturers by being able to provide customized materials at a fraction of what it cost to do the same thing in America. What remains in the US market are smaller operations which can provide smaller orders with faster turnaround times on short runs that the foreign Asian markets cannot handle. Minimum orders for Asian textiles begin in the thousands of pieces.

Mass customization has the advantage over mass production in that vast storehouses are no longer needed when customized orders can be produced on demand. Its avowed goal is to eliminate manual setup that results in greater speed of production and delivery. It has had some notable and expensive failures. Levi's attempted a customization project where individual women could get measured and have custom fitted jeans delivered to their doorstep. The project was discontinued as a complete marketing disaster. Proctor and Gamble spent six years and $60 million on customizing cosmetics for individual women. The project was finally cancelled. Still more and more companies are giving customization a go. Mars Candy is cautiously proclaiming success at manufacturing individually customized M&Ms. Even though one bag of the customized candies costs five times as much as a regular bag, they have been selling well. Customization in any manner is antithetical to the lower costs and lower prices that should result from mass production and economies of scale. Mass and customization are at opposite ends of the production process. Thus, the phrase "mass customization" has all the markings of a fad management theory.

There is no doubt that mass customization is having its effect on the marketplace. The idea is intriguing, especially for those companies and individuals who can afford the higher prices and have customers who are willing to pay more. It certainly for the moment has its place in expanding markets. The question remains, however, if this is the prize that produces the new business model. A review of history suggests that it is not. Assembly line manufacturing did not become the definitive answer to business success. Mass customization is just a spin off of the assembly line model, and it is doubtful that it will perform any better in the long run. What it amounts to really, is simply an effort to utilize current technology, which is well and good. At the end of the day, however, when the technology has been mastered, the same problems of profitability remain. In short, when everyone is using the new technology, the playing field will return to square one.

If it's Bigger, it's Got to be Better

As of this writing, General Motors may no longer hold the title of the World's Largest Automobile Manufacturer. Size alone does not guarantee successful business as quarter after quarter GM sales have dropped repeatedly. As already discussed in Chapter Two, efforts to increase the size and revenue of a company through mergers and acquisitions have for the most part proven to be unsuccessful. It simply is not a business model that produces steady profits. In the great majority of cases, overgrown companies have only succeeded in destroying stockholder value as they mismanaged and then shed their once promising acquisitions.

Divestiture after incongruous acquisitions continue to point out that bigger is not necessarily better. When Altria Group acquired Kraft, Inc., it looked like a major coup for the owner of Phillip

Morris Tobacco Company. Early in 2007, however, Altria spun off its Kraft division. The explanation given was that the spin-off would give Kraft the opportunity to make relevant acquisitions to its already impressive portfolio: well known and respected brand names such as Oreo, Jell-O, and Oscar Meyer. The reality, however, is more likely the inability of management to run two disparate businesses. Once again, increasing size and diversification did not deliver the expected results.

> **"The purpose of business is to make a profit by supplying customers with goods and services that they want."**

Many small businesses also start out with their eyes on the wrong prize. These business owners think ahead to growing their businesses even before they have entered a market. Moving a home-based business into a rented office with all the office trappings before the time is right is almost guaranteed to create a negative cash flow from too much overhead and too little business. This simple fact can also hold true for successful businesses that try to expand too soon. Overexpansion, even within your core business, can be disastrous. So imagine the low probability of success when expanding into unrelated industries. Recent history also points to the fact that large companies that swallow up smaller ones not actually related to the core business make no sense. A company grown into a ponderous, disjointed conglomerate is not likely to increase profits. Usually, when a parent company buys up other, disparate businesses, all companies become less well managed.

Promises, Snake-oil, and Miracle Cures

Just as many large businesses have been lured into expensive management fads that end up costing much more than first estimated, do not function as expected, or simply get abandoned after a short time, the promise of business growth through innovative technology lures many businesses into growth schemes.

It is tempting for a small business to turn to a company whose marketing plans, designers, consultants, and expert management personnel are guaranteed to grow its business. The bottom line is that all those experts come with a price. If profitability is not in the picture already, growth will not come from added expenses of growing the company. The end result will only be a larger, unprofitable company. If hiring professional consultants appears to be the way to go, business owners and managers would do well to interview prospective consultants carefully to see if their eyes are on the right prize.

Rightsizing for Improved Cash Flow

A less negative impact word than downsizing, it still amounts to the same thing. There are times when right sizing is dictated by economic and political situations. For example, downsizing certain operations was necessary with the outbreak of World War II. Sometimes, downsizing is necessary when a company has lost a great number of customers as a result of regulatory fiat, natural disaster, or political turmoil. These situations are few, however. Downsizing is almost always necessary because of bad management. Logically, a dysfunctional large company will only be a dysfunctional smaller company after downsizing unless other changes are made as well. What downsizing usually amounts to is having management's eyes on the wrong prize. The thinking might go something like this: We grew too fast and cannot keep up with the market we attracted; therefore, if we become smaller and leaner we will be all right. Unfortunately, it is usually an oversimplification that is based on tunnel vision.

Rightsizing is acceptable when it is the result of careful study on how to improve a company's performance. The view should be based on how the company became oversized in the first place. What management did that created the problems the company is now facing. In today's marketplace, a large part of the problem has been because management and CEOs concentrated more on shareholder profits than they did on building the business. If the company could boost stock prices and therefore satisfy shareholders, less attention was paid to cost cutting and optimizing production. Many times announcing a reduction in the labor force serves just such a stock price increase.

Rightsizing is mistakenly considered superior to fixing the real problem which is usually loss of sales. It may appear to be well advised where, for example, a large contract is about to be fulfilled and there is no new contract waiting to take its place. Since the payroll is a current liability, a sudden reduction in payroll can provide an immediate boost to cash flow and therefore can bump up the stock price. But, you can't downsize your way to prosperity. You also can't continue to cut payroll until it is zero and then expect to make a profit because your costs are so low. Downsizing is a crisis management strategy that may help the short-term survival of the company. But, if the downsizing does not address the reasons for the scaling back of the company, the company will continue to be dysfunctional-just at a smaller size.

> ***Downsizing is almost always the result of mismanagement.***

The truth about rightsizing is that in many cases it does not really reduce expenditures at all. Large companies that have laid off thousands of employees (such as in the airline sector) often end up hiring consultants, independent contractors, and temporary workers who are the very people that were let go. Humorously, some examples of downsizing have been termed "dumb sizing." Dumb sizing is defined as downsizing that did not accomplish what it set out to do.

Some downsizing begins to take on the look of corporate moves to make the next quarter's earnings look better for shareholders. This suspicion if raised when large companies lay off large numbers of staff during December and January. If net income for a current year does not look all that impressive, in the beginning of the next quarter the ledger sheets will improve considerably after a large reduction in the workforce.

Downsizing may also begin to look like a corporate tool for use in management/labor confrontations. From the 1980s when downsizing began to gain momentum as a management tool, a greater percentage of the labor force began worrying about losing their jobs. It is possible that downsizing has also been used as a scare tactic to keep labor costs in check. When workers are worried about the jobs, they are less likely to agitate for higher pay and greater benefits.

Once again, the business of downsizing appears to be an instance of not having the corporate or business eye on the right goal. Like so many other so-called business tactics, the practice becomes a kind of corporate game rather than a serious effort to increase value through improved production which brings about steady growth.

Attracting the Wrong Investors

CEOs, directors, and share holders alike seem to overlook the obvious fact that stock prices are volatile and subject to both internal and external factors. Management is usually quick to take credit for upticks in stock prices. But watch the stock price fall, and the finger pointing begins. The fingers typically point to external factors beyond the control of management. When investor focus is on those wonderful surges in stock prices, all too often the almost inevitable stock price drop in the business cycle is forgotten in the euphoria. The short term stock investors are not interested in the long term growth of a company. They are in the business for a quick turnaround on their investment dollar without concern for the overall health of the company.

When a company has its eye trained on short term investors, the corporate games of big announcements and (sometimes inflated) splashy earnings statements take both time and resources away from the steady, common sense growth strategy that long term investors are looking for. A company focused on its stock price is tempted to "manage" earnings for the sake of the next quarter's results. The company is also making itself vulnerable to charges and lawsuits for corporate fraud. The temptation to inflate numbers and under report losses has given us the Enrons and the WorldComs of big business. Focusing solely on today's stock price is another example of having your eyes on the wrong prize.

Looking for Miracle Workers

Here's another problem with the cult of personality known as the celebrity CEO. Celebrity can trump other selection criteria when recruiting a top executive. This is another example of having your eyes on the wrong prize. It is rare for one person to be able to rescue or save a company. Even a sole proprietor who labors under the mistaken idea that he or she can do it all is living in a fantasy. Nevertheless, the need to hire someone often causes a board to finish the business of hiring a new CEO as quickly as possible without doing the due diligence they would put into purchasing a new car. Some of the questions unasked in the hiring process include:

- What expertise do the candidates have in our business?
- What track record do the candidates have in the area of team building? Many of us still admire the lone wolf or the self-made man.
- What exactly will the candidates bring to the company— flashy headlines or sound business sense?
- How flexible are the candidates in their vision and their management styles?
- What expectations do the candidates bring to the table, and are those expectations realistic?
- Are the candidates more interested in their salaries, stock options, and severance packages than they are in learning what the company needs?
- Are the candidates willing to tie their rewards to company performance?

Perhaps no one in recent memory has pinpointed the silliness of corporate America better than Scott Adams in his cartoon strip,

Dilbert. Management with eyes on the wrong prize is satirized by characters called Dogbert and Catbert, and inept middle management consistently has bad hair days. The immense popularity of the strip should give management more than a chuckle. One thing that consistently comes across in Dilbert is that rank and file employees often have a clearer picture of what the company actually needs than does management.

Vague Images

Incredibly, lists of some business objectives fall into the category of eyes on the wrong prize. Not only do they miss the mark, they are abstract and have only remote bearing on what is really important. Take, for example, the common business objective of "improving customer satisfaction." What precisely is the definition of customer satisfaction, and how much do we have to improve it to be considered successful? An easy way to accomplish higher customer satisfaction is to reduce all your prices. Customers are happy consumers even though your company goes broke. So customer service cannot be a stand alone business objective. Serving customers must include making a profit. Otherwise you are running a charity and not a business.

Usually such vague business objectives are simply a symptom of not having a real target in sight. Suppose NASA set "space" as its objective in the Mars missions. It would be an accident of incalculable odds if one of its probes actually landed on the Red Planet. This is one of the major faults of business fads-getting so absorbed in the process that the end result, the ultimate objective is ignored or never even considered. Business objectives should be centered on bottom line considerations rather than some immediate goal to improve a process or streamline a function. Business plans, like most mission statements, that have no explicit and quantifiable goals are just wishful thinking. They are not serious business strategies. And they almost always fail.

Looking for Solutions in All the Wrong Places

While looking for the brass ring of success, many companies make the mistake of looking for it in someone else's company. There are no two companies in which the same business model works identically. There simply are too many extenuating factors involved. Cultures and personalities differ; company objectives may not always be the same; leadership qualities are almost certain to be different. Once again, such a practice indicates a lack of clear vision. Even when a new business fad seems to work well in one company, it fails miserably in another.

What works in one company may even hinge on such things as compliance with government and industry regulations. A new IT system in one company may be able to produce a measurable result while in another company it may not. The new system, once installed, may work well and expedite the flow of information, but it is usually an oversimplification to attribute success or failure of the business solely to the new system. This kind of blind sight overlooks other important factors such as changes in management, downturns in the economy, the exit of a major competitor from the market, or any number of possibilities.

Like so many of the other business missteps we have covered in this book, the tendency to look for answers in all the wrong places is simply a desperate search for the quick fix. Both research and analysis need to go into looking for solutions to business problems. This means research within the company, analysis of what is being practiced, and whether or not it is doing the right things instead of doing the wrong things right. A business consultant who approaches the task with common sense rather than disruptive new systems will be able to accomplish this task. The consultant can serve as an objective analyst and keep management grounded. All too often, however, it is the consultant who is the instigator of and the biggest cheerleader for the latest business fad.

Looking for Solutions Before Understanding the Problem

If management jumps in with solutions before fully understanding the problem/s/, their eyes are also on the wrong prize. It is like giving an answer when no one even knows what the question is. There is no argument that solutions must be found to business problems. There is likewise no suggestion that business will run along for years and years without problems. What is at question here is the practice of coming up with solutions without properly analyzing the current business situation. That takes patience which is further proof that there really is no such thing as a quick fix. Furthermore, solutions of themselves are not the ultimate focal point. Call it what you will—company direction, company vision, company goal—solutions to any business problem must be aimed at furthering the true aim of the business. A solution to any problem will also bring about change in some way or another. That is the desired result of a solution, but looking only at the result of a problem solved is yet another example of wrong sightedness.

Looking only at solutions may preclude observing other factors such as risk. Many IT solutions might never have been started if the management had evaluated the risks involved in making such a drastic change. Furthermore, solutions to problems should be measurable. A solution that produces no measurable difference is no solution at all. Only by first really understanding the problem can a workable, measurable, and relevant solution be achieved.

Innovation for the Sake of Change

Most people are aware that Southwest Airlines didn't just start the low-cost, low-fare segment of commercial aviation. Southwest also perfected it. The company has continued to make a profit even while other low-cost airlines joined the major airlines in going broke. Starting from its hub in Dallas, Texas, Southwest was able prosper while maintaining a point-to-point model in contrast to the industry's hub-and-spoke model. Moreover, it has retained its dominant position in its particular niche for thirty-odd years.

Southwest Airlines' business vision was based on innovation not in hardware or computers, but in the way they viewed the customers and the customers' travel needs. Southwest's eyes were on the right prize. By contrast, Coca Cola's attempt at innovation in 1985 was one of the major marketing disasters of the century. Part of the new business plan was to update the main product. It was not change based on customer demand, but change for the sake of change. Coca Cola's new formula was an internal decision imposed on the external environment-the customers-instead of being driven by those customers. The results were disastrous.

One of the latest trends in corporate business is another addition to what may already be top heavy management: the CIO. This is the newly designated Chief Innovation Officer, not the Chief Information Officer in IT. Companies including giant soft drink manufacturers and large banks have jumped on this bandwagon which looks like a lot of the other quick fix fads of recent years. There is a real danger with adding such a position that other people in the company will develop the attitude that innovation is "not my job." It's doubtful that one person can somehow lead innovation in all the departments of a modern corporation. It is also doubtful that adding another department to a business will in any way improve the core business strategy of the business as a whole. Finally, the idea of "innovation spending" as a way to increase business already shows signs of having the eyes on the wrong prize.

Square Pegs into Round Holes

There is no question that innovation throughout an organization is not only desirable; it is usually mandatory. That's because the world and its markets are constantly changing. To stand still is to regress relative to your competitors. The point is that innovation must be the servant of the business rather than the driver. There are hundreds of thousands of patents on file that represent new technology but have little commercial value. The technology is neat but has no useful purpose. If something new with a fancy name (or acronym) comes along and requires an altering of the business to fit the technology, something is seriously wrong. It is an attempt to fit the square pegs of business into the round holes of technology.

One of the latest ideas of large corporations is using technology to allow customers to contribute ideas now called "open innovation." This may be a noble idea, but it is hardly something new. The tried and true way of gathering innovative ideas is on the showroom floor or on a sales call. Prospect preferences are not at all the same as customers' purchasing behavior. Going back to the example of Henry Ford, the drop in sales happened when Ford failed to observe what the customers were saying. How might history have been rewritten if Ford had listened to dealers who told him that people were going down the street to buy a more expensive model because they wanted a blue or red car? Customer preferences cannot be determined in the executive suite, by marketing surveys, or in focus groups. These are all just starting points. Customer preferences are gleaned from actual sales. The truest test of a customer's sincerity is when he opens his wallet and hands you his money.

Open innovation (otherwise known as listening to your customers) does not require another Vice-President. That, however, is what some many companies are now doing. There is a trend of creating new departments or divisions at the top levels of management. In this case, the motive may be noble, but the means of achieving it are questionable.

The struggling American automotive industry is a classic example of not listening to consumers. Since the energy crunch of the 1970s people have expressed interest in automobiles that were 1) reliable and well-made, 2) fuel-efficient, and 3) stylish. Instead, the American auto industry has consistently produced lower quality vehicles with poor gas mileage and me-too designs. It does not take a Vice President for Innovation to observe buyers' preferences. It has been no secret what the public wants, but the U.S. companies have resisted those preferences. In early 2007 Japanese auto makers had 7 of the 10 best selling models in the United States. In the hybrid category, American car makers have perennially dragged their feet despite clear indications that the public wanted these vehicles. One of the auto makers excuses for not making hybrid vehicles has been that they are more expensive to produce. The result has been that American made hybrids are an insignificant part of the product mix. Meanwhile, Toyota and Lexus have together sold more than 500,000 hybrid vehicles here.

Advertising is Not a Business Plan

As a stellar example of failure that came from the reliance on advertising to do the job, the Government Accounting Office blasted the Office of National Drug Control Policy (ONDCP) for its ineffectiveness and waste of government money on media ads. The ads were designed to educate America's youth and lessen the use of controlled substances. There is evidence that the ads had the opposite effect. One might argue that the ONDCP is not a business and, therefore, the comparison does not apply. But, we would argue that ONDCP is a business in the sense that it is trying to influence customer behavior vis-à-vis the consumption of drugs. The organization is in the business of trying to stem the problem of illegal drug usage in the country. This is another example of a bureaucratic solution to a problem. Run some ads, but do nothing of substance to achieve the organizational goals.

Whatever hopes were pinned to the splashy ONDCP media ads went unrealized and unfulfilled. Corporate advertising has had similar results. Back in the 1980s the Coca Cola Company spent a huge sum-even by Coke standards- on its "I'd like to buy the world a Coke" campaign. It did, in fact, spawn a hit song, but the sales figures did not show a significant increase.

Now, in the 21st Century, we are seeing dotcoms as they dot bomb, having made mistakes as old as commerce itself. With fixated eagerness, they accepted the popular opinion that web commerce is the wave of the future. In the frenzy many basics were completely overlooked:
- Inattention to customer service
- Inability to fill a great number of orders in a short time
- Failure to recognize that a company's ecommerce success may hurt its dealers or retailers

- Lack of expertise in actually getting product into customers' hands
- Failure to create delighted customers who become good will ambassadors for the company

Websites and ecommerce have certainly established themselves in business. But, they are just tools. Ecommerce is another sales channel. It is not the business. If your product is poor, your customer service is surly, or your company is understaffed, a website is not the answer to your business success.

So What Works?

Throughout the first half of this book, we have been highly critical of the way many businesses are run. Please bear with us. We recognize that criticism without solutions is pretty worthless. So we have dedicated the last half of this book to recommendations for creating higher profits, happier employees, and more satisfied customers. There are some business basics that have been proven to work through the years in all industries. No fads, no buzz words. Just sound business principles and people serving people.

Keys to this Chapter

🔑 We too often get wrapped up in process over goal. A recipe is not the food.

🔑 For any new idea, ask the question, "how do we make money from this?"

🔑 There are no miracle workers. It takes teamwork.

🔑 You can't downsize your way to prosperity.

Chapter Five

The End of Loyalty

Not that many years ago it was common for a young adult to graduate from high school, work for one company for the next 30 to 40 years, and then retire with a nice pension. There was employment security for both employer and employee. Employers benefited from low turnover; and employees were secure in the knowledge that their jobs were permanent and their incomes reliable. Today, that job security is vanishing. Today, workers all across America come to work each day wondering whether they will have jobs next month or next year.

Admittedly, today's workers are more mobile in their careers. Younger workers are not very interested in that lifetime employment. They want opportunity, advancement, interesting work, and high starting pay. They care much less about job security and pension plans. And they will change jobs and companies more readily than previous generations to get these things. Some workforce experts have estimated that the typical worker in her 20's will work in 8-9 jobs during her career. Changing jobs or employers has no stigma for this generation. In fact, most younger workers assume they will change jobs every 3-4 years for whatever reason. So it's understandable that employers would have little loyalty for such transient workers.

The reality is, however, that the loss of loyalty started with employers. Over the last forty years, employment in larger corporations has followed the boom and bust cycle of acquisition and divestiture we have seen in the U.S. Companies grow faster than management can keep up with the resultant overstaffing and under training. The following downsizing is accompanied by layoffs. Employees are considered expendable. In many companies employees are just an input, much like equipment or inventory. Too much inventory? Sell it off at a discount. Too many employees? Pay them off-through severance pay-to reduce the workforce and "right size" the company.

This casual regard for the workforce may make accounting sense, but it creates significant long-term problems for the company.

- The lack of job security causes many of the most valuable employees to leave to work for companies where they have better long-term employment prospects.
- The lack of job security discourages prospective employees from considering the company as an employer.
- It's impossible to determine exactly how many people should be dismissed. The initial cost savings can be calculated, but the drop in productivity and total output becomes known only months after the layoffs.
- Typically, each department is told to cut payroll by a fixed percentage. However, some departments were overstaffed, some understaffed. The layoff creates an even greater mismatch between work staff and workload in each department.
- Morale of the surviving workers is ravaged. Productivity declines as remaining workers become preoccupied by their own job insecurity. Additional layoffs reinforce their worries.
- In many cases, cost savings are less than originally estimated because of severance and continued benefits paid to laid off workers. So a lot of good people are now jobless for little real benefit to the company.

- When management realizes it has lain off too many people or decides to "grow" again, it goes back into hiring mode. Most of the laid off people will not return. They have moved on to other employers. So the company has to recruit new people and suffer the time and expense to train the new hires. Even if you disregard the human cost of the layoffs, the financial costs to the company are significant.

- Finally, layoffs represent a failure of management to hire properly, train adequately, and keep sales up to keep employees busy. If the company does not undergo serious self-evaluation with corrective action, reducing the workforce may cut costs temporarily. But, by itself, reducing employment will not fix what is wrong with the company. The overstaffing is symptomatic of much larger problems within the organization.

Some companies have recognized the wisdom of keeping morale high in the workplace and have succeeded in keeping internal operations running smoothly with minimal employee discontent. In far too many companies, however, the attitude that employees are disposable has become the norm. Long term employees live under the implicit threat of being replaced by younger, less expensive workers. Layoffs in the tens of thousands are constantly looming on the business horizon. Downsizing or rightsizing are terms workers hear daily on the news. Bankruptcies resulting from poor management or outright fraud have become commonplace. People see their pension funds wiped out by corporate mismanagement while bungling CEOs walk away with millions of dollars in severance pay. It is no wonder, therefore, that employee loyalty to the companies they work for is at an all time low.

> *In far too many companies, the employees are considered disposable.*

The One Way Street

It is commonplace for big businesses to harp on company loyalty to the employees. Signs, posters, and pep talks from management emphasize the need for employees to be loyal to the business. What management usually means by that is never complain and do not look for a better paying job. Employees are not impressed by such a posture. As many workers see it, that is a one-way street. Management wants my loyalty, but I am expendable at any moment. Another man relates an instance when he had been offered a higher salary in another business and he went in to tell the CEO that he would be leaving the company. The CEO berated him severely and he left the office feeling almost like a traitor. Not two weeks later, that same CEO announced that he had accepted a position with another company and would be gone by the end of the month. Employees learn quickly that loyalty is expected from rank-and-file employees, but it does not apply to upper management. It is a one-way street that is clearly erected for the benefit of management with no reciprocal loyalty handed down.

The Fallout Effect

Over the last decade, corporate scandals rocked the nation and the nation's workforce. So many workers were affected that the stories were given considerable ink and air time in the popular media as well as the business press.

- HP's CEO was alleged to have been involved in illegal electronic spying on the company's own board members as well as on their contacts in the media. Employees who knew they would be fired for any hint of illegal activity observed that a company double standard seemed to exist.

- Enron Corporation collapsed in a maze of creative accounting, insider trading, management lies, and massive fraud. Employees saw their life savings wiped out while company management remained millionaires.

- Accounting irregularities at Fannie Mae that allowed top executives to receive multimillion dollar bonuses were brought to light. Criminal charges were filed.

- In addition to the mismanagement at Firestone Tire that led to the largest tire recall in history, the company was found to be using child labor at its rubber plantation in Liberia.

- When the Ford Pinto was proven to be dangerous because of a design flaw that caused the car to burst into flames during a collision, a somewhat callous management concluded that recalling all the cars and correcting the problem would be more expensive than simply settling the lawsuits that had been brought against the company. Rational financial accounting perhaps, but a public relations disaster for Ford. Both Ford employees as well as the rest of the nation saw the value Ford management placed on human life.

- Accounting irregularities at Parmalat International masked serious mismanagement. When the books were corrected, it became apparent that the company was insolvent.

- CEO David Edmondson of Radio Shack was discovered to have lied on his resume, claiming a degree that he had never earned. Rank and file employees in all companies know the consequences of filling out false information on job applications.

- In 2003 the Dennis Kozlowski scandal at Tyco came to light over a $6,000 shower curtain in his ostentatious New York apartment. Other instances of massive misappropriation of company funds were discovered at the top. In most companies, taking paperclips or ball point pens for employees' personal use is grounds for dismissal.

- In 2002, accounting fraud at World Com overestimated the company worth by about $11 billion. The company went into Chapter 11 bankruptcy. Many of the top managers went into prison.

Now you could argue that these executives got what they deserved. They were found out and punished, weren't they? The problem is that it took years of investigation by government agencies to uncover the scandals and effect corrective measures. The wonderment of it all is to ask the question, "What were the other senior executives and directors doing all this time"? There will always be bad characters in any industry. But the real scandal is that there appears to be very little self-policing or self-correction in the executive suites of corporate America. This feeds the notion among average Americans that all executives are crooks. Imagine what it does to the employees who actually work for these companies. If the top executives are leaders and role models-and we believe they are-it's scary to think of the effect these scandals have on the average worker. Some of them will use these bad behaviors to justify their own greed and selfishness.

Business Ethics

In the 1970s Lockheed Martin was caught up in an ethics scandal that involved paying kickbacks to foreign entities to obtain contracts. Shortly thereafter Congress passed the Foreign Corrupt Practices Act, but Lockheed Martin had already taken major steps to incorporate ethics training into its program. Scott Adams was recruited to add *Dilbert* cartoons to the company's training materials. In the intervening years, Lockheed Martin has, in fact, lost out on contract bids when the only way to get them was through kickbacks and bribery. In a time when the names of Enron, Tyco, World Com, and many others are on almost everyone's lips, Lockheed has set a positive example. Boeing paid a hefty $1 billion fine after it was discovered that an employee had pilfered proprietary information pertaining to an Air Force missile contract.

When companies like Lockheed Martin include ethics training for everyone from the CEO on down, employees are reassured that double standards within the company do not exist. In the long run, such programs improve employee loyalty to the company. Employees want to be proud of the companies and their leadership.

Disposable Employees

Different companies value their workforces differently. But in all of the following examples there is a management mindset that the employees are just another input to be increased or decreased according to business conditions. Interestingly, the idea of disposable employees is not limited to management. Other company employees may be infected by the same thinking.

- **Management's disregard for workers' health and safety** may seem like a scene out of 19th century sweatshops. But the example of Tyler Pipe, a cast iron foundry in Texas, suggests that workplace safety is not a priority in at least one company. Tyler Pipe, one of the world's largest manufacturers of cast iron pipe, has been characterized in print and on television as one of the most dangerous places to work. The company has allegedly disregarded safety precautions that have resulted in thousands of injuries and even a few deaths. Tyler Pipe has been cited for health and safety violations resulting in fines. In 2005 the company pleaded guilty to two felony charges brought by the EPA.

  Throughout the media coverage the company has been characterized as the most dangerous place to work in America. The company seems to have only grudgingly upgraded its employee work policies and pollution control efforts. The point is not to single out one company, but again to demonstrate the low morale and productivity that result when a company resists making positive changes on behalf of its employees and even the community. Most of the corrective actions seemed to have been forced upon this company's management by government agencies including OSHA and the EPA. It is short-sighted management that ignores workers' health and safety until forced to improve conditions through fines and prosecution.

- **When management treats workers as just hired help** the employees soon recognize their status as disposable employees. It also becomes apparent that this attitude starts at the top of the organization food chain. It is a throwback to medieval times when workers were considered little more than chattel to serve the whims of aristocrats. This disconnect is exacerbated when senior managers have their own private dining room while the average worker eats in a dining hall that has tile floors and plastic chairs. Often, workers do not even know what the people in upper management look like. The workers recognize their leaders only from photos on the walls. This us-versus-them mentality reveals itself in loss of employees' loyalty to the company and its mission.

- **Legal loopholes that make employees disposable** are used by many companies under the guise of downsizing. Because it is a lengthy and sometimes cumbersome procedure to summarily dismiss employees, the company can claim downsizing and eliminate any number of people. Employees do understand if the layoffs result from external circumstances that the company has no control over. However, in many cases as the "downsized" employees are shown the back door, new employees are pouring in the front. Morale among the remaining workers sinks as it becomes obvious that older, higher paid employees are being replaced by lower wage entry-level personnel.

- **Temporary workers are by definition disposable.** Temps are being utilized more and more for that very reason. Hiring temporary workers is appealing to management in a number of ways. An important reason for the surge in temporary staffing is that the temporary workers can be discarded at will without the legal processes necessary to remove permanent staff. Need a worker for a day or week? Now you can rent them instead of buying them through permanent employment. Furthermore, many of the temporary employees come highly qualified since they are often made up of skilled employees who were previously downsized. Delta Airlines hired back many of the employees it had let go as temporary contract workers. This may make short-run financial sense, but how motivated and loyal are workers who are here today and gone tomorrow?

- **Staff disdain for temporary workers** may have a negative effect on productivity. Full time employees who suddenly have to share their workspace with temporary hires may often resent the intrusion. It is also common for permanent employees to look down on the temps as disposable employees. And since there is no real incentive for temporary workers to have any kind of real loyalty to the company, that attitude is likely to spill over in the workplace.

- **"At will" hiring** is another factor that contributes to a lack of employee loyalty. Everyone understands that an employee who is hired on an "at will" basis may be terminated at any time for (almost) any reason. But "at will" employees still have some legal protections. Even an "at will" hire cannot be dismissed on the basis of discrimination or because of filing a workman's compensation claim. Still it is much easier for management to dismiss an "at will" employee than one under contract. But most employees see "at will" as a legal concept that does not apply in the real world. Most employees consider their employment to be fairly long-term, if not permanent. It is not unusual for these employees to develop a great sense of loyalty toward the company that gave them jobs in the first place. When management exercises its right to dismiss them suddenly, and especially when the employee had no idea it was coming, serious damage is done to loyalty and morale among the entire workforce. It sends a clear message that loyalty to the company will not be reciprocated.

- **Reliance on disposable employees as a business model** began with the fast food industry and seems to be spreading into other sectors. It may be a resignation by management that these employees are working starter jobs and will soon move on. Nevertheless, this managerial mindset can backfire on the company. The employees that are considered disposable or short-term employees are the same employees who come into direct contact with the customer. These employees are the company to the customers. Providing excellent customer service ought to include putting your best people-the people with the best interpersonal skills and most positive attitudes-in positions that have customer contact.

Motivating Employees is Unnecessary

Ask almost anyone who has just been hired how they like their job and the company they are working for. In nine out of ten cases, you will get a glowing report. Employees usually start to work in any new job with a positive attitude and motivation to do the best job they can. Ask those same people what they want from their jobs and likely you will get the same, or at least similar, answers. Employees want to be treated fairly, they want to enjoy the people they work with, and they want their work to be recognized.

Six months later, ask those same questions of the same people and do not be surprised if the answers are less than enthusiastic. A year later, some of the attitudes will be right antagonistic. If you are objective, you can understand what happened. Management has failed. Instead of maintaining the motivation and enthusiasm of the new employees, something in the management style has instead demotivated these workers.

To be treated fairly, employees want fair pay and benefits, but they also want recognition for work done well. Raises and bonuses are no substitute for recognition and appreciation. Management needs to realize that both rewards are necessary to maintain employee morale and enthusiasm, and to foster employee loyalty.

Employees are not impressed with speeches by the CEO about the employees' being the company's greatest asset. That is especially true when the next week scores of employees lose their jobs to downsizing. What management has overlooked is that there is no need to motivate already motivated people. The company needs to stop un-motivating them by unfair practices, condescending attitudes, failure to recognize individual work (or, worse, giving credit for individual work to someone else). Many employees can recall the indignation they felt when senior management gave full credit for a project to an inept middle manager who wrongly takes credit for his subordinates' work. Loyalty is well on its way out the window by that time. Likewise, benefits should be based on concern and compassion. Employees should not have to fight their own corporation's bureaucracy to receive their promised benefits.

Much has been written and umpteen seminars have been presented that deal with employee motivation. Many times this information centers on motivating the underperforming employees. Rarely does anyone ask how the employees got demotivated in the first place. Surely, the company didn't hire demotivated people with bad attitudes. Something has happened to destroy their zeal and enthusiasm. The answer almost always lies with management. But looking at it as a management problem is too painful for the bosses. So the company hires motivational speakers and sends employees to motivational classes. And management thinks it has fixed the problem.

> **"Downsizing, layoffs, and divestments all represent a failure of management."**

What Killed Employee Loyalty?

Employees' jobs are to get things done; management's job is to coordinate and to facilitate that process. In the best of all worlds, that implies a level of cooperation and mutual respect. Somehow the focus on today's business models has turned outward instead of paying attention to the need for keeping the internal wheels well oiled. One of the recent buzzwords, *synergy*, is most often applied to mergers and acquisitions. The dictionary definition of that word is the working together of two or more components where the combined effort is greater than the single effort of each part. CEOs eyes light up at the prospect of mergers where two different companies will combine forces to achieve bigger and better things. The reality has been, more often than not, just the opposite: the combined effort has been less than the sum of its individual parts. Still, CEOs and corporate boards continue reaching for that illusive brass ring.

In the process of pursuing these mythical external synergies, companies today have lost sight of the internal environment. Managers have never learned or have forgotten that synergy begins at home. If you can't get your own team to work together and be productive, how will you ever get two different companies-with their two different cultures- to do it? And if your management philosophy is to treat your employees like machines, what effect will that have on the newly merged employees? Perhaps the reason that the average employee of today will have eight or more different jobs during the course of his or her working life is that today's worker is no longer willing to put up with the lack of respect and appreciation by his bosses. He is willing to change jobs until he has found the work environment that treats him like a valuable asset.

There is also another problem with employer-employee relations. The self-centered and self-promoting attitudes of management today have translated into a what's-in-it-for-me generation of employees. Consider these commonplace scenarios in business today:

- Management sees sales slipping for various reasons. Its response is a slash and burn reduction in the work force. There are now fewer employees who are subsequently expected to maintain production levels that previously required more people. Employees are not stupid. If ten workers can turn out the same quantity and quality of work that it used to take twenty people to do, why were the extra ten hired in the first place? If twenty people were really necessary, how will the remaining ten ever hope to get the work done? More often than not a business downturn is the result of too little management rather than too many employees.
- Workers who have long years of service and higher than average salaries are suddenly laid off as management tries

to keep the company ship afloat. As a result of that action, the remaining employees become fearful of having any kind of job security and many of them start looking around for other jobs. Management wag their heads and complain about the lack of loyalty among the employees.

- Health insurance costs go up and management announces that the company can not afford to pay the higher premiums. Management offers the employees the option of keeping the company group policy if they agree to pay for more of it themselves. Employees rightly observe that management plans for increases in basic supplies and other costs. Then why did managers seem to assume that healthcare costs would remain constant? It's true that healthcare costs and medical insurance premiums have been rising faster than any other business cost. But it appears more than a little disingenuous to be asking employees to pay more while the CEO gets mega-bonuses. It does nothing for employee morale to reduce benefits in the name of poor cash flow while the company goes on a buying spree.

- When employees see that merit raises are few and far between, and annual cost of living raises are only half of the actual increase in the cost of living, they conclude that they are not highly valued by management.

- Management often seems oblivious to the fact that employees can read. When employees see that their CEO was given a pay raise and a huge bonus for the success of a project that was achieved through the efforts of hundreds of people, yet they go uncompensated, they quickly realize that there is little connection between effort and reward.

The bottom line is simply that employees want to be treated fairly. Synergy starts within. When there is no synergy between management and the employees, there is no company loyalty. Employees often readily admit that the only reason they show up at work is for the paycheck at the end of the month. But every company issues paychecks. If employees can move to a company where they get respect and recognition in addition to a paycheck, that is exactly what they will do.

What is Loyalty, Anyway?

Managers who talk about company loyalty are usually speaking of employees who will work extra hours when needed, come in early and stay late, or spend a weekend doing something for the company like repairing a machine or writing up a proposal. What they have in mind are employees who devote themselves to the business and whose only thought is what they can do for the company. Or, perhaps, they have the idea in mind of an employee who is so mindlessly loyal he will not leave the company for a better, higher-paying job. There is rarely a CEO or top manager who thinks of loyalty in terms of the company's being loyal to the employee.

True company loyalty can really be found in that employee who is true to himself. That employee will do his or her very best at all times, not because it is owed to the company but rather because it is who the employee is. Conversely, true company loyalty from the employee's point of view is a management that takes the time to really see who is doing what and makes sure the rewards are appropriate. Take the example of three employees doing the exact same job. Imagine that the two newest employees are doing the job to the best of their considerable ability. The third employee has been with the company ten years longer than the other two and draws a salary that is 10% higher. That employee, however, does inferior work and depends on the other two to complete projects. It is amazing that most management cannot see the inequity in such situations. It is even more amazing that management does not understand why the newer, more productive employees quickly resign and move on.

The Military Model Does Not Work in Business

The military model begins with a kind of humiliation that drills into the minds of recruits that strict obedience in a formal chain of command is the only behavior that will be tolerated. Furthermore, the underlings are a captive bunch. They may want to leave but they can not. They have no alternative but to do what they are ordered to do and little or no incentive even to think for themselves.

If Joe in the machine shop comes up with a cost saving idea that will be inexpensive to implement, why should he not be able to go straight to the top manager in his department? Why should he be forced to hand the idea over to a middle manager who will present the idea in the editorial "we" and grin when he is given credit for the innovation? Over and over again, employees see people who have never in their lives had an original thought get credit, praise, and even monetary rewards for work or ideas they were forced to hand over to a middle manager. Logic should tell CEOs and top management that such behavior is unfair and not conducive to getting the most out of the workforce.

The military model also works negatively in the reverse. If you get the picture of the general chewing out the colonel who blasts the major who scolds the captain who berates the lieutenant and on down the line, you see a fairly typical blaming chain in business. The bottom rung employee can only go home and kick the cat. Or, he can get busy and find another job.

Loyalty and Termination

Downsizing, layoffs, and divestments all represent a failure of management. But contemporary management practice consists of taking credit for all the good things in your company while denying any responsibility for the bad stuff. In fact, we have come to the point where managers are rewarded with raises and bonuses for correcting their previous mistakes. The term "layoff" is transformed by newspeak into one of a number of euphemisms. These euphemisms are just a smokescreen for managerial ineptitude. But companies continue to "down size" because it sounds so compassionate. And it makes management look like heroes for "right sizing" the company. The result is commonplace throughout corporate America: reward senior management when the company does well-even if the success is because of external factors. And reward senior management when things go bad. After all, they're fixing the problem, aren't they? We now have the amazing spectacle of senior executives getting bonuses for dismissing their own employees. Sadly, few observers seem to be bothered by this. The practice has become so ingrained in corporate governance.

It is also this kind of verbal subterfuge that makes the idea of company loyalty a joke. An employee does his assigned job. The company pays a fair wage. That is the beginning and the end of loyalty. When the top management sees the employee as disposable at company whim but expects that same employee to put the company before self, that is the logical outcome.

Loyalty is not something that is owed to a company. The only thing an employee owes to his or her company is a fair amount and quality of work for a fair salary and agreed benefits. Employee loyalty is not some reverence for the company that has magnanimously offered employment. Employee loyalty is not stupidly accepting wrong headed policies of top management. Compare the headlines: *Ford Announces 10,000 Layoffs* and the next one *Ford CEO Gets $28M for Four Months Work*. Or look at the P&G buyout of Gillette where the chairman and vice-chairman got severance amounts adding up to $228 million at the same time several thousand jobs were eliminated. It is incredible that more directors and stockholders do not act to correct these inequities. And it is galling that many managers still complain about the lack of loyalty among their employees.

Requiem

Employee loyalty did not die a natural death. Poor management killed it. Working conditions more than salary considerations cause many employees to jump ship at the first opportunity. An undesirable side effect of so-called job-hopping today is that it no longer bears the stigma it once did. Unfortunately, high turnover is common in the workplace today. But few realize that high turnover represents management's failure to take care of their employees.

Perhaps the saddest thing about the demise of employee loyalty is the effect it has on customers, as we will discuss in the next chapter. If a chain is only as strong as its weakest link, management has contributed to its own vulnerability by ignoring the value of getting good employees and keeping them. It has become popular to blame the home, the school system, and the Boy and Girl Scouts for the loss of employee loyalty in the workforce. The situation has become so bad that even the definition of employee loyalty has changed. Instead of finding employees who plan to spend their careers with one company, loyalty is now defined as employees who stay with the company for a year or two.

Management has also damaged employee loyalty by being blind to what is really going on "down on the floor." Morale sinks after management decisions adversely affect the working conditions. Most of the time those decisions are made from a lack of knowledge about the workplace environment. When management drags its feet by not responding to troublesome and unproductive employees, it is not the bosses who suffer. It is the people who have to work along side of the troublemaker. When management makes a decision to promote an employee based on tenure or seniority, instead of merit, morale and employee loyalty suffer.

Management has also been guilty of establishing one-way communication from the top down without setting up a means for employees to express their ideas to management. Let's call it the suggestion box mentality. Those contraptions used to be found in every shop and some offices. They failed as a means of communication when management decided the employees were not offering suggestions but were simply using the boxes to file their complaints. It did not seem to occur to anyone that valid complaints are also matters that need to be addressed. Employees soon noticed that the boxes were not even being opened and the idea died along with company morale and employee loyalty.

The dehumanizing attitude toward disposable employees has done major damage to employees' loyalty to their companies. Add to that absurd executive salaries, perks, and severance packages that make CEOs wealthy for life, and it is time to hold a requiem for employee loyalty to the company.

A Checklist for Top Management

- Communication should flow up and down the organizational chain of command.

- The best way to stop the us-versus-them mentality: everyone gets bonuses or none gets bonuses. The boss should not be paid raises and bonuses for getting rid of his employees.

- It is the duty of management to handle the problem of difficult employees. Do not allow rotten apples to spoil the barrel.

- Get out of the executive suite and see what is happening within the organization. Do not assume middle management is reporting the bad with the good. See for yourself.

- Pay special attention to the employees who have the greatest contact with your customers. In many organizations they are the lowest paid, least trained, and have the least seniority. But to the public, they are your company. They have a major impact on your brand, and on your customers' satisfaction. And unhappy customers create unhappy employees.

Keys to this Chapter

🔑 Employees' loyalty to their companies is decreasing.

🔑 New hires start their jobs motivated and enthusiastic-that's why they were hired.

🔑 Something has happened to demotivate employees and make them disgruntled.

🔑 Demotivated employees represent a failure of management.

🔑 It's difficult for employees to stay motivated when they see no connection between their efforts and their job security. Also, they see no connection between the CEOs efforts and his bonuses.

🔑 Everyone should share in the bonuses.

🔑 There should be no executive rewards for laying off employees.

Chapter Six

Chasing Customers Away

Everyone has had the experience as a consumer where something caused him to walk out of the business determined never to darken the doorway of that establishment again. It is the same when shopping online. You want to make a purchase, but the website is confusing. Or the form loses your data and makes you reenter your information. Or maybe you can't even find the order page. Something causes you to abandon the shopping cart and leave the web site. In most cases, the company is responsible. Rarely is a situation like that actually caused by the consumer, but rather it is caused by some policy of the business or some behavior on the part of the employees, or by a complication or inconvenience with the website. As many as 70% of customers abandon shopping carts on some web sites.

The Employee is the Company to the Consumer

Companies often fail to understand this basic truth: the employee a consumer interacts with during a transaction *is* the company in that customer's mind. The satisfaction of the customer is proportional to the satisfaction the employee has for his job. A customer who comes to buy is not dealing with a celebrity CEO or a marketing acronym. That customer is dealing with a human being. While online shopping is the ultimate self-service experience, eventually there will be a need to contact customer support and deal with a human being who represents the company. The success of that interaction is vital to the success of that business.

> *"Today, an unhappy customer can post online and share his complaint with thousands of people in minutes."*

Although the employee-customer relationship is given lip service in most companies, the reality is that little is done to see that it is first class in every way. The attention of management is too often on the "big picture" rather than down on the selling floor where the life blood of the business actually flows. One of the dangers of CRM, for example, is that the customer is reduced to a database record. Too many companies think business success means avoiding all human contact with the customers. Let the computers do it. Let the CRM program "manage" the customer relationship.

One of our clients recently told me about a bad experience he had with a store that is part of a nationwide chain. "I was in the store, waiting in a line of people. There were employees walking around all over the floor wearing headsets and looking very important. Even though there were more employees than customers, there was only one register open. So of course there was a line at the register. Somehow, the assistant manager got stuck working the register, and he was obviously unhappy about it. When it came my time to check out, he was impatient and rude. His face was contorted in a frown, and his tone was sarcastic. I decided that I wouldn't put up with that kind of treatment anywhere else and I certainly wasn't going to pay money for the privilege. So I put down my purchases and walked out of the store. When I got back to my office, I emailed the company's corporate offices to complain. A few days later I got a form letter apology in an email.

Some weeks later I decided to give the store one more try. Nothing had changed. My complaint apparently had been handled by a clerk whose responsibility is sending form letter replies to complaints. From now on I will drive farther to shop the competition."

He went on to say that he realized the few hundred dollars he spent there every month was just a drop in the bucket to the company. But he pointed out that this poor customer treatment, if repeated at stores across the country, would drive away thousands of customers and cause a sizeable loss of revenue. Now we recognize that store employees can have off days. The real insult was the tepid response from the corporate headquarters. An unhappy customer was giving the company valuable feedback, but the company just didn't care. Most of the time, dissatisfied customers leave quietly and never come back. Companies spend millions of dollars every year to try to find out what their customers are thinking. Managers should be delighted to get customer feedback-positive, but especially negative feedback-because this feedback is true market research. And, it's free. But in this case, an indifferent corporate staff combined with an insincere apology caused the loss of a customer and a lot of bad public relations.

There are two dynamics at work in cases such as this one. First, that man's image of the company is inseparable from the disgust he has for a rude employee. Second, the response he got from the corporate office was indifferent to his complaint. An apology from a nameless, faceless clerk in the head office with an impersonal email was both insincere and insulting. Had the manager of the local store called that man, he would have felt more like he was being treated as a valued customer. Instead, it seemed like company policy to chase that customer away.

Consider too that the rudeness of the employee is also a lack of loyalty to the company. He simply does not care what the customer thinks about the company. If the employee received any training on customer service or customer satisfaction, it had clearly been a wasted effort. The subsequent form letter from headquarters confirmed to the customer that the customer is really a nuisance to the company. The clerk was upset that he had to spend time taking a customer's money. The home office couldn't be bothered with a personal reply to a customer's complaint. All in all, this is a company that says, in effect, "Go away. We really don't want your business". Well, the company won. They lost his business, and probably the business of everyone he tells this story to.

You may have heard the adage that says, "A happy customer will tell 5 people; an unhappy customer will tell 20". That saying is obsolete. Today, we have websites, blogs, and email distribution lists. Today, an unhappy customer can post online and share his complaint with thousands of people in minutes. You would do well to reconsider what an unhappy customer really costs you.

My client went on to say, "Lately, whenever I've been at the checkout counter, cashiers have been asking me for my Zip Code. They enter this datum into their database before giving me my total. Sometimes I want to shout out that I am not a five digit number. I'm not even a five-plus-four hyphenated number. I have a wallet in my pocket, and I know how to use it." But then, I calm down and realize that they just want to update their CRM software. I am not just a number. I am a database record.

Daydream of the Perfect Product or Service

Some of the business fads are centered on zero defects in production. Companies have bought into the myth that products can be perfect. The problem is that people don't buy products. They buy benefits and experiences. First of all, everyone knows that there is no such thing as a product that will never break or a service that will always be rendered perfectly. Of course a customer wants to have as near perfect a product as possible. But the important consideration in the customer's mind is, "When something goes wrong, is the company going to take care of me? Will the company stand behind its products?" Cranking out products with a six sigma defect rate (3.4 defects out of one million pieces, which is actually 4.5 sigma's. But, hey, Six Sigma is an alliterative, snazzy label, isn't it?) is sometimes a small part of overall customer satisfaction. The company misses the big picture when almost all emphasis is placed on minimizing production defects. No matter how great the product may be, sales will suffer and customers will be unhappy if the total experience is unpleasant. The customer experience begins long before the actual sale. For many products and services, the total customer experience never ends. A major management mistake is thinking that customer satisfaction is solely product based.

- Do company representatives provide helpful product information in the pre-sale phase?

- How easy is it to navigate the company website?

- How many phone buttons does the customer have to push to talk to a human being?

- How quick and easy is it to actually purchase the product?

- What hours are you available to your customers?

- How long does the customer have to wait to get the product?

- How many colors does the product come in? Models? Sizes?

- Does the customer have any shipping options? Or do you ship your way?

- What does the company do if the product is DOA or breaks soon after purchase?

- How available is technical support?

- How available is the repair staff?

- How easy/difficult is it to return the product?

- How long does it take the customer to get a return phone call? An email reply?

- When do you repair; when you replace; when do you refund?

- When the customer is unhappy for any reason, what is your response?

- Who takes care of an unhappy customer?

Customers understand that things break. They even understand that they may purchase that one product that slipped through the QC inspection and has some defect. What they want is a company that will stand by its product and offer reasonable service to get the product repaired or exchanged. Almost everyone remembers when Sears maintained an active customer service department. Maybe Sears' products weren't state-of-the-art. No matter. People bought Sears appliances because they knew there were trained people available to work on their appliances when something went wrong. Parts were readily available. Repair service was prompt. There was a business model: sales people on the floor who knew the products backed up by a department trained specifically in servicing them.

> *"... people don't buy products. They buy benefits and experiences."*

Extended warranties are an example of a practice that appears to be good customer service. It is actually customer abuse and serves mainly to boost the retailer's margins. Some extended warranty plans began with good intentions. Years ago electronic components were very expensive, and difficult to repair. Parts were scarce and technicians had neither the training nor the support system to fix problems. Extended warranties that included replacement were sometimes advisable for early releases of new technology. Today, retailers attempt to sell extended warranties on just about everything in their stores. One retailer actually offers a warranty plan for only $4…on a ten dollar item!

The reason retailers push extended warranties is because the warranty plans are extremely profitable for the retailer. A $180 plan might cost the retailer only $20-30. Now we are business experts who believe in free markets. Even though we regularly consult with companies on pricing strategy, we are reluctant to criticize a company that wants to charge what the market will bear. But we see a bigger problem with the hard selling of extended warranties-two problems actually. First, to justify the cost of the extended warranty, the company has to denigrate its own product. Take the example of a new notebook computer. Extended warranties for notebook computers are pushed because the LCD screen could go out and cost $400 to replace. Or, the motherboard could fry. And a new motherboard could cost as much as the entire computer. In other words, the less reliable the original notebook computer, the better deal the extended warranty is. So the salesman raises doubts about the reliability of your product so he can up sell the add-on extended warranty? Second, the packs-the warranties, taxes, cables, and accessories-can double the original price. This may seem like good business practice and good sales technique, but we argue that it is short-sighted.

Customers go shopping with a general budget in mind. When they come to your store with a budget of $400 and they leave having spent $800, there's a good chance they have been taken advantage of. You made a good profit off the customer this time, but will the customer come back? Yes, he got a lot of stuff for his money. But, he also got more than he intended. We call it customer abuse-a type of financial rape. The customer goes home with an uneasy feeling, a type of buyer's remorse. And that makes it less likely he will return to your store for a future purchase. He knows (or thinks) that future purchases will cost him a lot more than he planned. The best way to avoid that situation is to avoid you and to avoid your store. You got a one-time sale, but possibly lost a life-time customer. You didn't really give him what he wanted. You sold him what you wanted. We argue that the sales process-including retail sales-should not be a win-lose contest between you and your customer. Selling one customer one time is what we call hit-and-run selling. You may make a lot of money from this one transaction. But, you will make even more from a life-long customer. And, life-long customers refer their friends; one-timers do not.

Treating Your Best Customers the Worst

The Holy Grail of most management is getting new customers. It is estimated that ninety percent of company effort consists of marketing for new customers. Sales, discounts, promotions, most advertising, special financing are at aimed at the new customer-the unproven prospect who may or may not buy and who may or may not become a long-time loyal, repeat customer. In addition, almost all the advertising budget is aimed at customer acquisition. It's common for companies to lose 10-20% of their customers each year. Some customers stop using the product, some die, but most switch to competitors.

Think about what it means to increase new customers by 10% while losing 10% of your existing customers. You have spent all that time, money, and energy on customer acquisition, but your total customer base is unchanged. If you're losing 15% of your existing customers each year, your business is actually shrinking. Furthermore, studies show that it costs ten times as much to get new customers as it does to keep your existing customers. So you can spend $100 to get a new customer, or you can spend $10 to keep a current customer. The result is the same. Yet where does most of the marketing money go? To customer acquisition, of course.

It appears that management in general has simply accepted the idea that over the course of a year twenty percent of their customer base will erode and the answer has been to get new customers. In other words, chase off twenty percent of our customers each year and spend inordinate amounts of money to win new customers. Bear in mind that we are talking about twenty percent per year. So the result is similar to pouring water into a leaking bucket. How many new customers coming in the front door would you really need if you could stop the flood of current customers going out the back door? This is why we are skeptical over the frenzy for growth that so many executives fall prey to. Generally, growth refers to new business, new customers, or new markets. However, it is far more efficient financially for your company-and better customer service-to spend some time and attention on the people who have been proven to buy from you and support you: your existing customers.

Devoting most of your resources to customer acquisition is a questionable market strategy that not only befuddles the minds of consumers; it is guaranteed to drive customers away. Almost everyone has had the experience of making a purchase and days or weeks later seeing an advertisement for the same product or service at a lower price. Great, the customer thinks, I have that, so I will be able to lower my monthly bill. Wrong. When the customer calls in to get the new deal, he is informed that the new, lower pricing applies to new customers only. The message is clear: we will move heaven and earth to get new customers; but once you sign on with us, you will be ignored and forgotten. People who have done business with the company for years see that their past customer loyalty means nothing at all to the business.

Where is the common sense in driving twenty percent of customers away, putting ninety percent effort and money into getting new customers, and insulting loyal customers? It looks like a classical case of diminishing returns. Marketing has thus become a giant game where loyalty is destroyed when only new customers can take advantage of "the deal." The obvious reward for being loyal to a company is a slap in the face, and at least twenty percent of those formerly loyal customers are in no mood to turn the other cheek. When the thanks for customer loyalty is paying higher prices, that is when the customer heads for the competition.

Antiquated Service Policies

So much has changed in recent years with the onslaught of modern technology. It has become not the wave but the tsunami of the future. Technology has changed our lives drastically and created a whole new playing field. Once a customer could buy a product and perform simple repairs himself. Unless the customer is an electronics engineer, he cannot do that any longer. And even if he is an expert in electronics, he has neither the equipment nor the parts to effect the repair himself. Most of us are helpless when our possessions malfunction. We are completely dependent on others to make our stuff work. This is further evidence that selling is no longer product based. It is service based. Whatever it is you sell, the customer wants to know that your company can be counted on to take care of him. Quick, quality service before, during, and after the sale is what the customer is looking for. But many companies still focus on the product. The problem is that every competitor has a product. And these products are becoming more and more similar because the technology is becoming universal. Knowledge is sharable and transferable. If you want your company to stand out from the competition in the 21st century, your competitive advantage has to be the way you care for your customers. Your emphasis needs to be on plugging the leaks in that leaking bucket, instead of just pouring more and more water in the top.

Cutting Customer Service to Cut Costs

It is not hard to imagine a few board members sitting around the table before the meeting begins and complaining about problems they have been having with the expensive luxury automobiles they recently purchased. A few moments later, those same people are looking at charts showing stock prices falling. They begin talking about what they can do about it. After all, as the prices fall, so does the value of their portfolios. Quickly they grasp for ways to cut costs, increase the next quarter earnings, and get those stock values back up. It is not an unusual scenario.

> *"... studies show that it costs ten times as much to get new customers as it does to keep your existing customers."*

Circuit City's solution to the problem is classic. Using average national wage statistics as their guide, Circuit City decided that its problem was that it was overpaying some employees, especially some of the sales people who actually have direct customer contact. These were the more experienced, more senior sales people who had shown some loyalty and longevity with the company. So, in a lead-up to April Fool's day, the company fired 3,400 employees nationwide. The terminated employees could reapply for their jobs at a lower wage, or the company would hire new people at the same lower wage. There is good news, however. Despite the company's financial difficulties, the President/CEO received a bonus of more than $700,000 in 2006. The company may reduce payroll costs through these layoffs, but the cost to the company could be far greater than any savings.

- The company intends to replace the experienced sales staff with new people who are, by definition, inexperienced and untrained.

- These laid-off employees were the contact points for the customers. Now the newest and least qualified people are going to be the face of the company.

- The severance paid to some people was reported to be the equivalent of 1-2 years of wage differential for the fired workers. In other words, the company might not see any savings for a year or more.

- There is a real cost to hire and train 3,400 new people.

- The 3,400 people fired are unlikely to be ambassadors for a company that replaced them with lower paid people.

- The firings sent a message to remaining employees that if you work hard, stay with the company, and master your job you will not be rewarded with raises for it.

- If you do get a raise, you will get fired.

Immediately after the announcement of the firings, some analysts were questioning the company's strategy. Granted the move would have a cost cutting effect, the analysts noted. However, the people leaving were the longest tenured employees who knew the stores, the products, and how to answer customer questions. Letting the most experienced employees go immediately raised the question of what effect that would have on the quality of service customers could then expect when they entered a Circuit City store.

Management complained that while they had been a front runner in electronic sales in the past, the competition had steadily eroded their market share and profitability. They saw the answer in making drastic cuts to their workforce.

The fallout from that questionable decision was immediate and scathing. At least one congressman wrote to the CEO rebuking the firings. Blogs started up on the internet that were anything but complimentary to Circuit City. Employees wrote about being informed at the morning meeting and immediately being escorted out of the building. Other employees wrote about how they were faced with being unable to pay their bills. Customers also weighed in with their own criticisms. Almost all of those ended their comments by saying they would never do business with Circuit City again.

In the meantime, according to company filings, the CEO of Circuit City was drawing a salary of nearly three quarters of a million dollars per year, receiving nearly that same amount in year end bonuses. He also had a long-term compensation plan that amounts to well over $3 million. Many people asked the pertinent question of why, if the company needed to reduce costs, did it not also reduce executive compensation and not just the wages of the hourly workers.

According to company announcements, more changes are in the works. It was announced that Circuit City's IT infrastructure is going to be outsourced to IBM. No comment was made on the cost of that or how much it would actually save the company. Meanwhile, there are more employees waiting for the axe to fall.

With the firings and the analyst predictions that profits would rise, the company stock actually rose by two percent. In other words, while many people were wondering how they were going to feed their families or pay off student loans, the value of the CEOs stock and options actually increased. One person wrote in a blog that it was absurd for executives to get paid for causing so much chaos. The public clearly sees what the directors turned a blind eye to. The reason Circuit City had lost market share had nothing to do with how the employees were getting paid. Instead of moaning over the drop in stock prices, management would have been better served to study the situation to find the cause of the drop and do what needed to turn it around. The customers were apparently never even considered in the process. This time the lost business may never be regained.

There is a larger issue here than just the misfortunes of these fired employees. Replacing these employees means that the company is reducing whatever emphasis it previously gave to customer service. As customer service withers, the selling process will become increasingly product based. Product based increasingly means price based. In effect, Circuit City has decided to compete on price alone. This is a very dangerous strategy. Only one company can be the cheapest. And there is almost always one company that doesn't know the principles taught in this book. That company will sell below cost in an attempt to gain market share. Selling below cost is a great way to gain customers. It is also a great way to go broke. If you are a company that is competing with another company that is selling below cost, it's a race to the bottom.

If this company needed to improve its customer service in order to regain its market share, letting the most experienced employees go seems like a curious strategy. This PR disaster ranks up there with Coca Cola's new formula. There is no profit in taking away what the customers like about a company and replacing it with something they neither want nor appreciate. That is completely ignoring the basics of customer service and, in the process, chasing customers away.

Reciprocal Loyalty

When employees feel that the business is loyal to them, they will be loyal to the business. The same is true for company/customer relations. Few people will tolerate a disloyalty. Traitors are held in utmost contempt. Yet in business, all too often the company turns its back on front line employees and customers.

Not that many years ago it was common to see bumper stickers on cars urging people to "Buy American." The foreign automobile makers were offering better products at better prices. Nevertheless, the American public responded loyally by buying

American cars. It was cultural more than economic, but even culture has its limits. Today, the foreign cars are here in even increasing numbers. The "Buy American" bumper stickers have disappeared. One of the main reasons for this situation is that while foreign (especially Japanese) manufacturers were focused on giving customers the quality and value they wanted, American manufacturers appeared to be focused solely on size and up sells. To this day, foreign cars come with few options. Most of the upgrades are included in the base price. One car: one price. American cars are a different story. Most American cars are available with dozens of options and hundreds of combinations. Adding most of the options can add as much as 33% to the base price. Your $26,000 car can easily become a $35,000 car. But, at least you got the car configured your way. What about the cars that you don't want in any configuration?

Once popular American car nameplates disappeared. The lame excuse GM offered for discontinuing the Oldsmobile brand was that it had the word "old" in its title. GM claimed that only older people were interested in buying the product and that younger people were going for the flashier, sportier foreign models. A reflective look at the Oldsmobile and its demise is a real puzzler. The car had a history of radical innovation and growing popularity in the market. Not many people recall today that Oldsmobile introduced GPS for automobiles. It would be impossible to list all the well-received innovations that came out of GM's Oldsmobile plant. It can be argued that GM chased the once loyal customers away by letting the brand lapse into the commonplace. While the mother company was focused on a stream of acquisitions, a car that had once held the third place in sales behind Chevrolet and Ford faded into oblivion. One cannot help but wonder what portion of the billions of dollars that were paid out in acquisitions would have kept Oldsmobile on the cutting edge. If Oldsmobile became "old," it was not because of the name. It was because of neglect. The customers had stated loud and clear that they liked the constant stream of innovation that Oldsmobile once represented. When that ceased, so did customer loyalty.

Gagging Good Will

Whether it's replacing older clothes, trading in a car, or prospecting for new customers, it's cheaper to keep what you already have. It's cheaper to take care of what you have than it is to buy new. Money spent fixing the clothes, repairing the car, or maintaining the current customer is always cheaper than buying new. That basic is overlooked all too often in spite of the research that confirms that it is cheaper to retain long term customers than it is to troll for new ones.

In fact, the bad public relations from lost customers is like tying weights on your feet just before a race. You put your company at a disadvantage from the beginning. New customers may hear customer complaints and be that much more difficult to win over. Even if a new customer is acquired, if that customer has heard disparaging remarks from friends, family, and associates, the connection is shaky. It is likely that the new customer is wary and ready to bolt at any moment.

It used to be said that if a customer is happy with a product or service, he or she may mention it to only one other person. But if the customer is dissatisfied, it will be mentioned to ten people. Look how times have changed. While management has fallen all over itself over IT technology as the wave of the future, it has overlooked another little aspect. As in the case of Circuit City, that one person who has something negative to say about a company these days is not limited to ten people. He or she gets on a blog and airs complaints that may be read by over a million people. Not only that, but in the downstream that follows hundreds more disgruntled people add their two cents to the negative publicity.

When companies chase away customers by relegating them to numbers, focusing on acquisitions or downsizing, or becoming fixated on company stock prices, they are damaging their good will. Unhappy customers are usually very vocal customers. Company policy towards customers that chase them away is a policy of investing in negative publicity.

Employee Loyalty Equals Customer Loyalty

We noted that in the wake of the Circuit City firings it was not just stunned and unhappy ex-employees who got on the blogs against the company. Customers jumped on that bandwagon in wholesale numbers. Although it is too soon as of now to tell if the massive firings will have an effect on profitability for the company, it is interesting to note that the original 2% rise in company stock ten days later had dropped to below where it was one day before the dismissals.

> *"Whether it's replacing older clothes, trading in a car, or prospecting for new customers, it's cheaper to keep what you already have."*

The message consumers have gotten is that the company only wants mediocre employees who in turn are expected to be able to offer only mediocre service. Nor is the first time Circuit City has pulled such a public relations blunder. Four years previously, it fired many of its commissioned sale staff (some 3,900 of them) because they were making too much money. That was under a previous CEO who later retired with a stock grant worth $24 million plus $4 million in cash. SEC disclosure laws make it possible to know that members of the head office inner-circle still get perks like $858 per month car expense reimbursement, financial planning benefits of about $6,000, and annual electronics benefits of $8,000. It appears that to maintain this kind of corporate generosity, financial security (let alone financial planning perks) has to be yanked out from under thousands of the hourly employees. So the public is left to interpret the move as an insult to employees. Anyone can see that employee loyalty to a company that uses such tactics is bound to be absent. Consumers are told by companies like this that disposable employees are good enough for them. That, however, is not what millions of people are reading on the blogs.

Gimmicks That Chase Away Customers

One of the latest fads to get customers into stores lately is to come up with gimmicks that appear to have real added value for the consumer. Appear is the operative word. These gimmicks come cloaked in fancy names such as "MVP", or "VIP". They usually involve yet another plastic card to carry around in an already overstuffed wallet. A customer may have just spent $379 for groceries, and gets a receipt that says he has saved $7.42. He may feel he has saved a little money. Or he may feel that the items were overpriced to begin with. And all the while the company gets to collect more data for its CRM system. No doubt many customers would prefer that the company lose the gimmicks and instead pass the savings on to the customers.

At many local pharmacies, their plastic coated, frequent-shopper cards usually offer discounts on products few people buy. Store coupons are the same. The coupons usually provide discounts for products you don't want. Ah, if we only had a better CRM system. We could then know what the customer wants before he does.

Gimmicks have proliferated so much that they have lost their power to get attention and to change consumer behavior. But companies persist in gimmickry. Perhaps the money would be better spent on customer care. That could be the latest gimmick. But that would require better training for our employees. And happier, more motivated, more enthusiastic employees. Whew! That's too much work. Let's just think up a new gimmick.

Misunderstanding the Nature of Purchases

Marketing has become so impersonal. It is nothing like the days when the owner of the general store often knew what a customer wanted before he or she asked for it. There was a good reason for that. Sam at the general store knew his customers. He knew what they wanted because he knew what they wanted to do with it. Today that is no longer the case. The customer has evolved into a statistic and the merchandise has turned into a model number.

Let's say a customer comes into a store to look at computers. Few salespeople, not to mention upper management, actually understand the motives of the customer. The customer is not really buying a computer- a box with a motherboard, a CPU, DDR RAM, and an active matrix LCD screen. He wants to send email, upload music or photos, create a spreadsheet for work, or a number of other things. Many employees are not trained to find out what the customer plans to do with a computer, or a chair, or even a set of golf clubs. Here is where conversation and good communication should come into play. Employees need to be trained to ask questions and listen carefully to the answers. If the product is a computer, a writer, a housewife, and an accountant will all have different uses in mind for the machine. The inner workings of the apparatus are just so many buzz words to most customers. What they want is the right machine to do the job they need to get done. That should seem obvious. But listen to computer salespeople give their pitches sometime. Observe the facial expressions when they discover that the customer does not know the difference between megahertz and margarine. So the salesperson sells features instead of desired customer experience and expectations. Or, the salesperson has to sell on price.

> *"Neglected customers can now tell thousands or millions of other people about your poor service."*

The customer comes in with two very clear things in mind. First, he or she has something in mind that the product will be used for. Next, he wants to know how the business will support him in the event that something goes wrong. Way back when, Sam at the general store either knew or asked the customers what they planned to do with the product, and if something went wrong, he would either get it fixed or exchange it for a new one. He never insisted on bringing back the sales receipt, the original box and packaging, or any of the other maddening things customers are required to do today to effect a replacement or return of a defective product. Sam understood his customers. Today, the frenzy for growth has turned every company into a mass marketer, and every customer into a database record.

Sam Walton, who built one of the largest companies in the world, did it by giving the customer what the customer wanted. He knew the people that made up his market and went after them with great prices, good quality, and friendly service. Recently, the company he built lost sight of that temporarily by adding an upper range line of designer clothing. They did have the good sense to cut their losses when it became clear that their customers would pay $300 for a stereo but would not even consider paying that for a designer dress. Whatever anyone may think of Wal-Mart, it cannot be denied that their accent on the customer—from the greeting at the door to the friendliness at the checkout—has worked to keep customers returning.

A Chase Nobody Can Enjoy

When customers abandon a business they have been accustomed to patronizing, they do not feel good. In some cases, when they walk out the door it is a matter of great inconvenience to them. It is much like the feeling of an old friend who suddenly turns a cold shoulder.

Management cannot really be happy when they have chased customers away. Endless meetings to brainstorm ways of increasing the customer base are not particularly enjoyable. The frustration of constantly pouring time and effort into refilling a leaking business is not a pleasant situation to be in. Stockholders are not impressed when profits sag, and the company is stagnating.

The disregard for long time and once loyal customers that are chased away is a losing game. It becomes the case where the company runs faster and faster just to stay in place. Sales growth is the net increase in revenues. That means the new sales you made less the repeat sales you lost. Given that the repeat sales are easier to make and cheaper to achieve, it just makes sense to spend more time and attention on your existing customers. Plug the holes in your leaking customer bucket. Then, all new customers will truly represent added business. That is the only true sales growth.

Keys to this Chapter

🔑 Companies rarely lose customers. If a customer has bought once, he has a certain built-in loyalty to the company. Companies usually chase customers away.

🔑 Most companies spend heavily to acquire new customers yet spend little to keep current customers.

🔑 It costs as much as ten times to acquire new customers as it does to keep your current customers.

🔑 Net growth equals the new customers you gain minus the old customers you lose. If you could reduce customer loss to zero, what would that do to your net growth?

🔑 Prospects have no opinion about your company. Current customers can be ambassadors for your company if treated well. Positive public relations, repeat business, and referrals: all free.

🔑 Neglected customers can now tell thousands or millions of other people about your poor service.

Chapter Seven

New Leadership

Substantial evidence exists that there is little correlation between executive compensation-salaries, bonuses, and stock options, and severance-and executive performance. When companies do well executives are rewarded with raises and bonuses. This seems to be independent of executive effort. In many cases company success is caused by external factors. Perhaps extreme weather wipes out a competitor. Or political events disrupt markets and create an artificial scarcity in the company's industry. Regardless of the cause, executive compensation rises with the good fortunes of the company. But there is still a disconnect between pay and performance.

Amazingly, the same thing happens when a company does poorly. Executive compensation still goes up. Sometimes, not as much as during good times, but up nonetheless. Sometimes, the justification is that the executives need to be rewarded and motivated to guide their companies during difficult times. No one seems to remember that it was usually the same executives who caused the downturn in the first place. Rare is the executive who declares that since the company is not doing well, he will forego a raise. Rarer still is the executive who refuses a raise because his employees are not getting raises or are getting laid off.

Today, executive compensation has been almost totally disconnected from executive and company performance. The executives not only accept this, they encourage this and even lead the effort to separate pay from performance. We have left the era of leadership. We have entered an era of Greedership.

Greedership is the emphasis by an executive on his own well-being regardless of the condition of his company. Greedership is looking out for Number One even while employees are losing their jobs or having their benefits reduced. And Greedership is milking a company for all you can, and then leaving before the company collapses.

We believe that Greedership is damaging to a company in a number of areas. First, because Greedership rewards executives all out of proportion to their contribution, it is damaging to stockholders, the owners of the company. Second, Greedership can accelerate a struggling company's demise or end whatever chance it had to recover. Third, to pay executives tens of millions of dollars, costs have to be cut somewhere else. The cuts usually come from a reduction in product/service quality which is not fair to customers. Or, the cost cutting causes employee raises to be reduced or eliminated. Sometimes, employees even lose their jobs. Finally, the disconnect between pay and performance is deadly to employee morale.

The situation is not hopeless, however. There are steps companies and their directors can take to make things right again:

- Directors need to realize that they, not executives, set policy and are responsible to the stockholders for overall success. The CEO serves them and the owners, not the other way around.
- Establish a true connection between pay and performance. Executives should not be rewarded when they layoff employees.
- If a company is losing money, reduce an executive's salary and/or eliminate his bonus.
- Require that part of an executive's compensation be in the form of company stock. Not stock options, but stock. And not in addition to salary, but as part of salary. He is now an

owner. If the stock price goes down, the executive loses money just like every other owner.

- Reduce or eliminate the emphasis on stock options. For start-ups that cannot afford executive salaries and would benefit from granting stock options do this: set the strike price at the average price over the last 12 months, or a rolling average over the last 6 months. This would stop the executive from choosing that one peak, atypical day to exercise the options.

Tunnel Vision

When CEOs, their directors, and their companies fall under the spell of the great Vision, sound business practices are often forgotten. The company becomes enslaved to a grand idea and persists in trying to implement it even as reality is screaming that the idea is dysfunctional. This tunnel vision accounts for billions of dollars lost when fad systems are implemented then abandoned when they fail to produce the Vision.

> *"Today, executive compensation has been almost totally disconnected from executive and company performance."*

Good management stays aware of all aspects of business rather than a single bright idea that promises the moon. Continuous improvement is not only desirable, it is mandatory for the company that wants to stay competitive. But no one method, idea, or practice can lead a company to greatness, nor can the Big Idea rescue a failing company. Slavish devotion to a Big Idea often leads to lower performance once the excitement of the new idea has passed.

Big Ideas can seem to produce positive results at first. This is mostly due to the Hawthorne Effect. This phenomenon was observed many years ago when a group of industrial engineers wanted to determine the effect of factory lighting on worker productivity. Each time the engineers increased the illumination in the work areas, productivity increased. Then the engineers decreased the lighting to further test the lighting-productivity relationship. Productivity went up some more. The lighting level clearly was not the factor. The cause for the rise in productivity was the attention paid the workers by the engineers.

This is what happens with Big Ideas. A manager reads a book or hires a consultant/guru who has the Big Idea. The manager gets inspired; his enthusiasm for the Big Idea spreads to his subordinates. Everyone is excited. People work harder. All the employees congratulate each other. The Big Idea is the answer, and the guru is a hero.

And then the excitement wears off.

There are still production problems. Customers still pay late. Meetings still waste peoples' time. Disillusionment sets in when everyone in the company realizes that the Big Idea cannot handle every situation. Worse, a lot of smaller problems were neglected during the reign of the Big Idea. Now, they're bigger than ever. The company is now primed for the next Big Idea. Surely, this one will work.

Out of the Executive Suite

Great CEOs are nurturing leaders and see themselves as servants of the company rather than feudal barons. The CEO is a coordinator, facilitator, hub, communications center, internal leader, and the external face of the company. The company does not exist for the benefit of the CEO. It is-or should be-the other way around. The focus should also be on the employees of the company, and especially on the customers.

When we say that the CEO is the face of the company, we mean he or she is the representative of the company to the world. He or she is the person most often quoted in print or seen on television during the business news. The employees also represent the company, but on a more individual level when they meet with customers. But there is only one CEO. What that person thinks, says, does, and gets paid have far more impact than anything any other employee does. That in itself makes the CEO the de facto leader and a role model. It makes a lot of difference whether the CEO is an aloof prima donna, or a shirt sleeves, hands-on guy who values teamwork and employees.

Great CEOs are not burdened with outsized egos. They are not consumed by stardom or outrageous salaries and perks, or seeing their faces on the covers of magazines. Under the new financial disclosure laws, annual salary packages including bonuses, perks, and stock options must be reported publicly. As a result of recent disclosures, we now know that some CEOs are being paid tens of millions of dollars. And they're getting this regardless of performance. In 2006, for example, the top ten highest paid executives were paid salaries ranging from $26,000,000 to $52,000,000. Other executives were paid even more when they resigned or were fired. A former CEO of Home Depot received a severance package of 210 million dollars. A reward for leaving the company worse off than when he started.

A look at the real world versus corporate America is something of an eye opener. In the military, for example, an experienced General makes about 11 times the salary of an E1 (private). In the Civil Service, a top executive will make about 11 times what an entry level GS1 draws. These are reasonable ratios. The President of the United States only makes $400,000 a year. Coincidentally, this is about 11 times the average wage in the country. Look, however, at salary ratios in the corporate world. Mulally of Ford draws a salary 400 times greater than an entry level worker. Nardelli, formerly of Home Depot, enjoyed a salary 1,100 times greater. One CEO in the oil industry was paid 8,000 times more than his average employee. The idea that one person is 400 to 8,000 times more important to a company than the typical worker is suspect at best. We acknowledge that CEOs do not vote themselves these amounts. The credit goes to the mindless and spineless directors who should be acting as the stewards of their companies.

Real Leaders Live in the Real World

There is the anecdote about a man doing some field work for a geologist in Dallas, Texas back in 1959. He was taking soil samples on several acres of undeveloped land near the Dallas Airport. While they were working, an Oldsmobile drove onto the property and four men got out to look around. They were about a hundred yards away from the man taking the soil samples. The man asked a coworker who those men were. They looked very important, at least the three men who wore expensive looking suits. The driver wore only a khaki shirt and pants. The coworker told him, "Well, I don't know who those guys are in the suits, but the man in the khakis is H. L. Hunt." In 1959, Hunt was considered to be the wealthiest man in the world.

> ## *"We have left the era of leadership. We have entered an era of Greedership."*

Warren Buffet, one of the world's wealthiest men today, lives in the same house he has occupied for 40 years. He reportedly purchased the house in Omaha, Nebraska, in 1958 for $31,500 and has never felt the need to move to a mansion. But then, Buffet was not born rich. He made his wealth through prudent investing, focus, and hard work. At a time when celebrity CEO salaries average about $9 million per year, Buffet's annual pay is $100,000. Moreover, Buffet has decided to give away something like $30 billion to charitable foundations while he is still alive. Typical of his down-to-earth practicality, Buffet reportedly said he did not want to leave his vast fortune to his children. He comment was that he would leave them enough so that they could "do anything, but not so much that they had to do nothing."

Buffet has been critical of Wall Street investment advisors who are compensated on volume as an end in itself. That might also apply to CEOs and boards of directors who keep their eyes on stock prices rather than the nuts and bolts of running a company. In fact, it could be argued that hiring celebrity CEOs at exorbitant salaries and mindlessly adopting fad ideas is simply a ploy to boost share prices. When Warren Buffet takes over a company he sees as a good investment, he maintains a hands-off policy in running the acquired company. His involvement is limited to completing the management team and basing management compensation on company profits. Following this formula has made him billions of dollars. Most people would agree that he has been successful. Yet many companies are still hiring CEOs and giving them unbelievable salaries and perks that are not tied to company performance.

It's important to point out that there is a vast difference between the accumulated wealth of people like Warren Buffet and Bill Gates of Microsoft and that of CEOs who are handed large shares of company stock simply to sit in the corporate office. Buffet and Gates are the major shareholders of their own companies. They founded or grew the organizations they built. Their net worth is the result of their enterprise. CEOs who are given shares of company stock just for their star quality have no real vested interest in their companies at all. That distinction seems to have been lost on directors who practically throw money at executives to manage their companies.

> ## "Great CEOs are not burdened with outsized egos."

Bill Greehey of Valero Energy built his company from the ground up with a philosophy of hard work, intelligent acquisitions, company teamwork and high morale. He also believed in spreading the wealth. Today, Valero Energy is near the top of the Fortune 500 list with annual revenues of over $30 billion. Contrast that with another Texas energy company, Enron. There the Greedership of top management brought the company into total collapse. The officers at Enron damaged the careers of thousands of employees and laid waste to the retirement funds of thousands of other people whose had invested in the company.

Pitney Bowes is another company where leadership, not Greedership, is the norm. This is an example of a company that took the necessary steps to adapt to a changing market. Originally a company known primarily for postage meters in the days before computers and the internet, Pitney Bowes moved into the IT mainstream by providing software, hardware, and solutions to manage mail flow. The company is famous for its attention to customer care as well. With over $5 billion in annual revenues, Pitney Bowes is on the fortune 500 list and ranks in the top ten of companies that produce computers and office machines. A large part of the company's success has been its ability to redefine itself and exploit technology to satisfy customer wants and needs.

Sam Walton, founder of Wal-Mart, drove the same old pickup truck even after he made his first billion dollars. The vision of Sam Walton lives on after him: provide items that customers want, keep prices as low as possible everyday, be sure that stores are stocked with those items, and treat customers well during their shopping experience. Although Wal-Mart has experienced fierce opposition to its expansion in the United States, the primary criticism of the company is that its prices are too low! In some peoples' minds, this is a bad thing. There have rarely been accusations of illegal activity or unfair trade practices. Except for those low prices, darn it. After fifty years of growth and success, Wal-Mart is the largest company in America. Its sound business methods plus its ability to adapt to changing markets have created its market dominance.

One of the oldest companies still in operation in America dates back to 1901. Harley Davidson has experienced a number of highs and lows during its long history. It virtually created the motorcycle market and was the dominant manufacturer for decades. It owned the market and was able to fend off competitors for many years because of its emphasis on producing motorcycles that were made in America. In 1969, just when motorcycle sales were starting to explode, the company was bought by AMF as part of that company's diversification strategy. Perhaps this is starting to sound familiar.

The new owners concentrated on lowering costs, mass production, and streamlining the product line. AMF also laid off many of the workers in an effort to cut costs. AMF made the same mistake many companies make when they take over another company: they think they can manage the business better than the previous owners. The result of AMF's reengineering was an output of very expensive bikes that were inferior to the foreign motorcycles that were starting to penetrate the U.S. market. Finally, in 1998 new owners bought the company. These new owners were bike lovers, not bean counters. Their strategy was to retain the classic styling of the Harley, while adopting the latest technology from around the world. They marketed the Harley Davidson name and created brand extensions with products from belt buckles to Ford trucks. But in addition to smart marketing, the new owners also brought proven business management methods and restored Harley Davidson to its leadership in motorcycle manufacturing.

Mighty Oaks from Little Acorns

To see Walt Disney Company today, you would hardly believe that the company started in a $10-a-month rented room in the back of a real estate office. Walt and his brother Roy did not have visions of the grand company that is so omnipresent in the world today. After their first animated film, *Alice in Cartoon Land*, was a big success, they concentrated on growing their business by providing audiences with the best entertainment they could create. Although Walt Disney has often been called a visionary, he was very much in touch with the tastes and trends of the times. Walt was quick to recognize the appeal of live action films and television production. It might be said that Walt Disney pondered his way to greatness, building a company of dedicated people working together to make Disney Studios a real powerhouse in the entertainment industry. Yet his success was not the result of some grand vision of empire building. He just wanted to produce the best cartoons and movies he could. He began with one animated film that grew into an industry. It was a business strategy of measured growth within an industry that everyone knew and understood well. This is an example of business that is both focused beyond profit and at the same time in pursuit of profit. Although Walt Disney was fixated on providing wholesome family entertainment, he was not blind to the necessity of making the company profitable. Each step in the growth of Disney Studios created its own contribution toward the profitability of the company. It is ironic that the later attempts to grow the company by hiring celebrity CEOs ended up costing the company rather than producing profit.

A Picture is Worth a Thousand Words

Looking at a photograph of Colleen Barrett, President of Southwest Airlines is like looking at a picture of someone's mother. Barrett had the very bad luck of stepping in as Southwest President just a few months before the attacks on September 11, 2001. Prior to 9/11 many of the country's airlines were losing money. Their load factors were falling; and the average age of their airplanes was increasing. In short, the airline industry was in serious trouble. The drop in air travel after 9/11 turned trouble into catastrophe. Colleen Barrett stepped up to the plate and started hitting home runs with the public. Days after the 9/11 attacks, Barrett assured the flying public that Southwest had taken steps to see that there would be no long waiting lines for flights despite the increased security measures at the nation's airports. Under her leadership, the employees of Southwest made good on that promise. Southwest passengers were delighted to find minimal delays and disruptions. Barrett also reassured the employees who watched as workers at other airlines were laid off. She assured them that reductions in workforce would be the absolute last resort if the company needed to cut back. It didn't. No layoffs were necessary. But Barrett's concern for the company employees paid off in company pride, employee loyalty, and a continued commitment to excellence. Since the government started collecting data on customer complaints against the airlines in 1987, Southwest has consistently had the fewest complaints.

Barrett's philosophy is based on the Golden Rule. She admits that mistakes are sometimes made. But she insists that those mistakes are opportunities for learning and improving. She also believes that businesses should take the initiative, especially in times of trouble, and that leaders should listen to their hearts. Southwest Airlines is perennially recognized as being the best run airline in the United States.

People First Leadership

Regardless of the size of the company, an emphasis on people, both employees and customers, is the foundation of good leadership. In some cases, like Google's founders Larry Page and Sergey Brin, the management style may be somewhat whimsical but still have the desired effect. Their success as a company is undeniable.

Another atypical CEO who has led his company to impressive growth is George A. Zimmer of Men's Wearhouse, Inc. He is passionate about focusing on customer satisfaction as the best way to attract and retain loyal customers. He refuses such current trends as conducting drug tests for prospective employees or running criminal background checks. Full time employees earn an extra three weeks off on top of their regular vacation times every five years. Store managers receive the same bonuses that higher paid managers get. Recently, he succeeded in recruiting guru Deepak Chopra to the company's board of directors to contribute ideas on team building and social responsibility.

Zimmer acquired Moore's Clothing for Men in Canada not for empire building, but as part of a sound growth strategy. First, Moore's already had a large market share in Canada, and it would have been foolish for Men's Warehouse to go head to head with Moore's on its home territory. Second, Moore's operations were very similar to those of Men's Wearhouse, Inc. Thus, the companies were very complementary. Finally, leveraging MW's existing strengths and expertise, Zimmer is planning to expand sales to include bridal gowns to complement the company's existing tuxedo rental service.

In addition to his people-first approach, Zimmer has kept costs down by locating his stores away from the high rent malls. He also narrates Men's Wearhouse television and radio commercials. His stores intentionally avoid the high-end boutique look, instead creating a more relaxed atmosphere where men are more comfortable. Such a decision indicates that Zimmer knows his customers and gives them what they want. The results have been spectacular.

Leaders Wanted: Ego Not Required

A "leader" cannot lead if no one follows. CEOs can insist on certain behaviors on the job with the implicit-or often explicit-threat of job loss for failure to perform. That is authoritarianism, not leadership. And employees put up with authoritarianism only as long as they have to. As soon as they find an escape, they're gone. The effective leader, however, will inspire employees to perform voluntarily. And the easiest way to inspire behavior is to model it. When children play "Follow the Leader" the followers do what the leader does, not just what the leader says. Leadership means acting the way you want your subordinates to act. It follows, then, that a true leader is not separate from his team. A true leader is part of the team. With leadership, the leader shares the same successes and failures as does his team. With Greedership, it's us versus them. With Greedership, the interests of the CEO and executive team are different from the interests of the rest of the employees. Many times, the interests of senior management are diametrically opposite the interests of the other employees, such as when the CEO gets a bonus while employees get laid off.

> *" Leadership means acting the way you want your subordinates to act."*

A truly inspirational leader will inspire people to look beyond their own self interests and aspire to something bigger than themselves. Ritz-Carlton has been very successful in inspiring its employees to become part of a hospitality team that is famous for its superlative customer service. Most employees prefer working on teams to working alone. Teams can accomplish bigger things. And good teams develop an esprit de corps that is energizing and gratifying. But the CEO has to be perceived as being part of the team. Otherwise, there is eventually division and resentment among the rank-and-file employees.

Teams are most effective when they share the work and share the rewards. This is as true in business as it is in sports. Teamwork makes everyone in the business a winner. Valero's Bill Greehey always insisted that if he got a bonus everybody in his company got a bonus. This share-the-rewards attitude was a major factor in the company's rise from nothing in 1980 to top-twenty in the Fortune 500 ranking today. CEOs like George Zimmer ignore industry norms and grant sabbaticals after five years of employment. Zimmer also sees that store manager bonuses are equal to upper management bonuses. Zimmer doesn't just talk teamwork; he practices it everyday in his company. Colleen Barrett treated Southwest Airlines employees as colleagues by openly discussing the difficulties the company faced after 9/11. This sharing and respect made the employees feel like partners and strengthened the employees' dedication and loyalty. The end result was to maintain the company's status as America's favorite airline. When CEOs escape the isolation of the executive suite and practice what some experts have called MBWA-Management By Walking Around-they send the message that everyone in the company is on the same team. It's not us versus them. It's just us. That philosophy of us and team is perhaps the most effective way to retain loyal and enthusiastic employees. And loyal and enthusiastic employees create loyal and enthusiastic customers.

Accepting Responsibility

Leaders avoid making excuses for business failures. The public has grown weary of corrupt executives pointing fingers at others or claiming ignorance about a company's distress. President Harry S. Truman modeled accountability for the nation with his famous "The Buck Stops Here" sign on his desk. A CEO who claims that he or she had no idea about what was happening in the business has just admitted his incompetence. He deserves neither his pay nor his position. He has cheated his employees, the stockholders, and the customers.

CEOs who remain isolated from their employees also cause other problems for their companies. This isolation also tends to insulate these executives from what's really going on in the sales department and the factory floor. They are dependent on middle managers for status reports. All too often the middle managers tend to emphasize the good news and downplay the bad news. And when bad news is presented, it's often the messenger who gets shot. Aloof and isolated executives hurt their companies more than they know. Effective leaders stay in touch with their employees, their customers, and their industry. A leader without accurate information is an ineffective leader.

Good leaders also understand that authority must accompany responsibility. If subordinates are to be responsible for certain tasks or projects, then they must have the authority to carry out the assignments. But, good leaders realize that they can never completely outsource their responsibility as leaders. Leaders are ultimately responsible for everything their team does. That is why good leaders make sure that they provide good coaching, regular feedback, and recognition. It's Truman's "The Buck Stops Here." Great CEOs delegate authority and responsibility, but they realize that it is still their responsibility to supervise and provide corrective feedback. "Delegate and forget" is common in the business world, but it doesn't work.

Accepting responsibility involves the ability to put the interests of the business ahead of personal interest. It is a matter of commitment to making the company work. Accepting responsibility involves being a mentor rather than a boss. It means caring and helping people to achieve their very best. In short, good leaders grow people while they're growing their companies.

Good Leadership is Adaptable

There was a time when the head of a company conducted his affairs the same way day in and day out, year after year. Those days are over. In today's fast-paced, ever-changing world the status quo is status woe. Some changes are adopted voluntarily when they are seen to improve working conditions or profits. But most change is external and involuntary. If the company is to survive, changes in products, processes, or markets are required. The key here is adaptability. Changing business conditions are a given. The legal and political environments change. Even the team changes. The staff you have next year will be different from the staff you have today. All of this requires that senior management be able to adapt their leadership styles as the dynamics of both business and employees fluctuate.

> *"A truly inspirational leader will inspire people to look beyond their own self interests and aspire to something bigger than themselves."*

Adaptable CEOs realize that they do not have to be involved in all levels of decision making. Adaptable CEOs do not micromanage their companies. They gather information and delegate appropriately.

How to Spot a Great CEO

A Supreme Court Justice once said, "I don't know how to define pornography, but I know it when I see it". Similarly, we may not know how to define a great CEO but we know one when we see one. These are some of the traits of great CEOs and great leaders:

- Great CEOs have earned the right to lead others because of their personal character and trustworthiness. Southwest Airlines did not fall apart after 9/11 because Colleen Barrett was a calming influence and had earned the trust of the employees.

- Great CEOs exude confidence and enthusiasm for their companies' products or services. That confidence and enthusiasm permeates the entire company. Great CEOs are the biggest cheerleaders of their companies. But, the cheerleading is sincere. Contrast Enron executives sending memos to their employees falsely telling them that the company was sound with a CEO who walking the halls in his company and developing rapport through one-on-one relationships.

- Great CEOs demonstrate steadiness in times of crisis. Those CEOs understand the need for keeping clear heads during dark times so that the employees are assured that matters are under control. People naturally look to leaders during crises. The way leaders conduct themselves can be stabilizing and inspirational for the entire company. If these CEOs have previously gained the trust of their employees, they can more effectively lead their organizations in bad times.

- Great CEOs understand human nature and do not over react during emotional storms. They have what some call high emotional intelligence. They can see beyond the present and visualize the big picture.

- Great CEOs understand deeply the nature of the businesses they are leading. This contrasts with the penchant of some boards to hire superstar CEOs who have no industry experience.

- Great leaders do not make changes just for the sake of change. Some people call this lobbing hand grenades. Apparently, a few business gurus advocate stirring the pot once in a while as an antidote to complacency. Adaptability is one thing—it is necessary to keep up with the times—

but sudden change for no clear reason has a demoralizing effect on employees. Great leaders understand that you do what works. If your game is working, you keep working that game. Consistency in leadership also inspires loyalty in employees and customers alike.

- Great managers lead by example. To paraphrase an old poem, "I'd rather see a lesson than hear one any day; I'd rather someone walk with me than merely show the way." Great leaders do not ask employees to do anything they would not do themselves. If leaders insist that employees be punctual for meetings, they themselves do not come waltzing into the meeting whenever it suits them. The leadership by example model requires the leaders to set their egos aside and be servants of their companies. This, then, is yet another reason why leadership and celebrity CEOs are incompatible.

- Great leaders are not ashamed to admit they were wrong and someone else was right. Nor are they reluctant to give credit where it is due. Just as citizens are disgusted by sanctimonious politicians who refuse to admit a mistake, employees also lose confidence in a CEO or manager who refuses to accept responsibility for his errors and shortcomings. In short, a great leader will attract and retain good team members because they are a reflection of his leadership.

> ***"Great managers lead by example."***

From the Ground Up

Since 2001 UPS has utilized an Employee Opinion Survey to allow all workers in the company the opportunity to be heard. The survey response rate has ranged from 86-89% of the total workforce. The purpose of the surveys was to create a dialogue between management and employees and to promote a customer oriented mentality throughout the company. By addressing areas of employee concerns, the surveys encouraged individual involvement in company policy. Management gets a clear idea of what the employees are thinking. This employee feedback, combined with the resulting changes, develops an atmosphere of teamwork. One benefit of such attention to employee input was a reduction in driver turnover by shifting the responsibility of loading and unloading trucks from drivers to dock workers. By listening to all employees, the company was able to better distribute the workload and increase productivity.

Leadership and Customer Awareness

In many companies the CEOs and boards of directors are focused only on the next quarter's earnings report and on the next day's stock price. Great leaders understand the simple idea that if the focus is on the customer, the stock price will take care of itself. Leaders who exhibit the characteristics of greatness inspire employees to react enthusiastically with customers thus turning the first time visitor into a repeat customer. It should be obvious that if there are no customers there is no business. But, too many companies treat the customer like an intrusion. Great leaders understand that the customers are the reason the company exists. The customers pay all the bills. Great Leaders are able to communicate the importance of customer relations with the people who actually interact with the buyers.

A buzzword of the 1990s was "value for money." To many company leaders that only meant quality of product. Customers do want quality products, but they will shop elsewhere if they do not get quality of service. Instead of worrying about their next bonus or a slide in their own celebrity, great CEOs keep the focus on the customer relationship. It has been estimated that 80% of customers who never return do so because of indifference on the part of the employees. Great leaders insist on a sales force that is enthusiastic, sales people who know the company products, and representatives who are never impatient or hostile with a customer.

Excellent customer relations are not accomplished with a quick training seminar. It is accomplished by leaders who demonstrate a real concern for customers and who lead by example.

> *"Great leaders understand that the customers are the reason the company exists."*

The New is the Old in New Clothing

Despite all the new books, seminars, and DVD's released every year, there is really nothing new about great leadership. The principles and practices may have new names and clever buzzwords, but what has worked for decades-even centuries-still works today. To be a leader is to be a role model. Leaders don't motivate; they inspire. They understand that they lead only with the support of those who follow. Therefore, leaders are servants who make sure that their followers feel valued, heard, and respected. A leader is really a member of a team. And teamwork beats selfishness when it comes to grand achievements.

Keys to this Chapter

🔑 Greedership has replaced Leadership. Too many executives put themselves ahead of the mission, the shareholders, and the customers.

🔑 Great CEOs are servants and stewards of their companies. They are members of the team.

🔑 Great Leadership means leading by example-being a role model. It means modeling the behavior you want from your employees.

🔑 Managers motivate; leaders inspire. Great Leaders inspire people to do more than the people previously thought possible.

Chapter Eight

It's the Profits, Stupid!

Each of us has bought a do-it-yourself kit at one time. Maybe it was a piece of furniture or a bicycle. The assembly manual probably made little sense to you, so you followed what you could and ignored the rest. Likewise with the pieces; you used all the parts you knew how, and discarded the leftovers. And the item actually worked. Sort of. Running a business can be just like that.

Since there is no assembly manual for your business, you create what is called a business plan. You keep the plan in a file or in your head, but it is your guide to running your business and making a profit. The sections you don't know-maybe finance, inventory control, or employee motivation-you just gloss over. Sometimes, in the excitement of entering new markets, increasing sales, or buying other companies, there is one special piece that is constantly left over. This piece is put aside until the realization sets in that this piece was not only important, it was critical. That piece is profit.

The business situation gets out of control for two reasons. First, management downplays the importance of profit, especially in high growth businesses. Second, management has been trying to control the wrong parts. When companies focus on stock prices, manipulate shipments and inventory to bump up the next quarter's earnings report, or "manage" earnings to meet analysts' expectations, they are caught in a fool's game. Everyone has seen big pushes to make the numbers in one quarter followed by loses in the next quarter because the juggling acts were not sustainable. In many cases, it appears that the rollercoaster ride was an attempt to manipulate financial results for a quarter so that management would qualify for bonuses or be in the money on their stock options.

There are many factors that affect the price of a company's stock. Natural disasters, war, government fiat, market changes, and political turmoil can all affect the operation and profitability of a company. These factors can have positive or negative effects. Moreover, these same factors can result in increases or decreases in stock prices, regardless of the underlying soundness or profitability of the company. In other words, CEOs have much less control over their companies' stock prices than they believe. A bad CEO can certainly run his company into the ground, destroying value and causing a severe decrease in stock price. But, there is no way even the most brilliant CEO can significantly increase his company's stock price quickly and make that increase long lasting. A stock price that spikes quickly will most likely drop just as quickly in the not too distant future. That is precisely why CEO compensation should not be weighted toward stock options. CEOs have far less control over their stock's price increase than most of them realize.

Historically, it can be shown over and over how an emphasis on short term earnings and stock prices has failed. It is a case of sloppy management or unjustified expansion that predictably results in over-capacity situations and over-staffing. At that point, with an eye toward the next quarter earnings statements, those companies compensate by selling off assets (often at a loss) and slashing the payroll. These are stop-gap measures, trying to counterbalance the company losses. The net result is not positive. Employee morale drops under the weight of job insecurity and lack of confidence in the management. People waiting for the axe to fall become indifferent and resentful. Such attitudes carry through to customers who begin to abandon the sinking ship. The very best employees scramble for the life boats as well. According to Leadership IQ, 47% of the typical company's high performing workforce is ready to quit or change jobs-today. Half of your best and brightest will leave you if they get the chance. But, only 18% of your low performers ever think about leaving. It stands to reason then, that companies playing the rollercoaster game by periodically dumping employees are going to turn away their best workers along with their worst. And if you lose your best people, you will lose many of your best customers because business is about people serving people. In fact, many of your best customers may be more loyal to your people than they are to your company. Do you have to tolerate the worst employees to keep the best? Not at all. You just have to find a way to make the worst employees better, and not downsize in the first place. Employees understand firing someone for poor performance. What destroys morale are the indiscriminate firings that occur during a periodic downsizing.

Businesses *can* control profitability, especially long term profitability. It is not as spectacular as sudden jumps in stock prices. It is just a matter of a fundamentally good business model cranking out profits year after year. That kind of steadfastness produces a measure of stability for employees, greater satisfaction among customers, and steady profits for shareholders.

Controlling Profits Needs a Clear Picture

There is an adage that says *if you don't know where you're going, any road will do.* This statement can certainly be applied to business. Individuals fail to achieve because they have no clear picture of how to get what they want. Most people indulge in wishful thinking that usually begins with "wouldn't it be nice if." It is like getting on a plane and thinking, "Wouldn't it be nice if we landed in Paris?" Unfortunately, many businesses seem to operate on the same mindset. There exists neither vision nor planned strategy. CEOs seem to run their companies with a "wouldn't it be nice" strategy.

The repeated cycle of acquisition-divestiture plays havoc with employee motivation and morale. Without a long-term strategy for long-term and sustainable profits, CEOs lead their companies on roller coaster rides of expansion and contraction. The one constant factor in this directionless business model is employee layoffs. When a company acquires another company, employees are fired to right-size the company and eliminate duplication. And when companies sell off subsidiaries, it's because the parent is in trouble, the subsidiary is in trouble, or both. In both cases, employees are considered an expense that must be cut to right the corporate ship. Massive layoffs should be unnecessary in business barring some major external calamity. Profits are important. Indeed, we repeat that the purpose of a business is to make a profit while serving customers. But eliminating employees you previously thought necessary means either that you were wrong to hire them, or that you don't know how to grow your business now. Either way, laying off employees to save money is a short term fix that rarely works in the long run because the layoffs do not address the real problem. The layoffs are a symptom of a deeper problem.

The concept of vision involves a clear description of what the business will look like in the future. The vision is an organization's preferred future. The vision should be written down, studied, and re-written until it becomes a clear picture of company goals. How an organization realizes its vision is the company's strategy. Many times, Vision is confused with Mission. They are not the same. The Mission of a company is a description of what the company is trying to achieve. Its purpose is why it is in business.

> ## "CEO's have much less control over their companies' stock prices than they believe."

We believe that most so-called business gurus have it all wrong. Either they don't understand their own gibberish, or they purposefully obfuscate. After all, if your guru speaks in arcane mumbo-jumbo and uses newspeak buzzwords, you think he must be really smart. He must have The Answer. You're too intimidated to doubt or question. Many companies spend thousands of man-hours and tens of thousands of dollars to create guru-led vision and mission statements. What they get are words on posters that are so banal and generalized that they have no meaning to anyone and are quickly forgotten. Take a quick survey of your own employees if you dare. Count how many-or how few-people know the company's vision or mission. Better yet, ask them if they know whether the company even has these.

Purpose, mission, and vision are worthwhile to ponder and to commit to paper. But make them simple, get them straight, and make sure everyone in a leadership position knows them and leads by them. Who decides what these declarations should be? The owners, of course. Either the owners directly in a closely held company, or the directors acting as representatives of, and fiduciaries for, the stockholders. It is a waste of everyone's time to have company-wide meetings where all employees suffer consultants who propound that a mission statement should be the product of company wide input. When a large group collectively writes a mission statement, it is reduced to the lowest common denominator. It becomes a useless statement that says nothing and means nothing. Besides, the employees should not be deciding the owners' purpose in investing their money in the company.

Most employees want jobs and paychecks. True, they want meaningful work. But their working for you is not their search for meaning. They are quite alright in helping you do meaningful stuff. They are also quite okay with helping you make a profit as long as they can be proud of the contribution they make. This is not a snobbish argument, nor an elitist one. Employees can be emotionally invested in their jobs. They want input into how they do their jobs. But, they come to you for employment because they want to be given a job. To use a military analogy, soldiers don't want to define the mission. They want to be given the mission. They will then carry out the mission to the best of their ability. Likewise, your employees want you to tell them what the mission is, and what your vision is. If you share these with them-and if the mission and vision are noble and worthy-your employees will do their jobs to the best of their ability. They will walk through fire for you.

The mistake so many leaders make is to essentially ask the entire company, "Okay, people, what do you think we should do? What shall be our mission and vision?" That's like a football quarterback kneeling down in a huddle and asking his teammates what play they want to run. There is only one quarterback, and he calls the plays. Deciding the company's mission and vision is not only the leader's prerogative, it is his responsibility.

The first and most important question any business leader or founder should ask is, "What is the purpose of this business?" This is not just some existential angst yearning for the meaning of life. This question is the heart of your business. It is why you do what you do. Once you have defined your purpose for the business, you now need to decide what it is you are trying to achieve. You now decide your Mission. Now that you have purpose and mission, you can look to the future to imagine what your company can become- a future size, place, or condition that fulfills your need to make a profit as well as make a contribution to mankind.

Let's use the example of a man who wants to start a pizza shop.
- **Purpose:** My purpose is to satisfy peoples' hunger for tasty pizza and make a profit for myself. (This is my reason for starting the pizza shop).
- **Mission:** To serve the Tribeca neighborhood (a neighborhood in New York City) with hot and delicious pizza in 20 minutes or less. (This is what I am trying to accomplish with my pizza shop).
- **Vision:** To become America's favorite pizza company. (This is what I want my company to become. It is short and to the point. It also implies I will be the largest pizza company in the country.)

It is not important that these written documents be typeset and framed. They could be written on the back of an envelope as long as they serve to keep the owner on track. The vision, mission, and purpose also help the owner clarify his business values-beliefs that will influence the relationships with everyone the business will come in contact with. And lest you think that the pizza man's vision, purpose, and mission are too limiting, remember this: a vision can be so future-focused that it is demotivating. Decide a purpose, mission, and vision that you believe in. Then, share your mission and vision with people who will help you achieve them. Along the way, you can always (and should) revisit your mission and vision periodically to redefine them as you become increasingly successful.

What are being expressed here are basics that everybody knows but most people tend to forget. Except for lottery winners, there are no accidental millionaires. And surveys show that most of those overnight millionaires ended up losing everything and being in worse shape than before they won the money. Most millionaires don't set out to make one million dollars. They did have a purpose; they did carry out a mission; and they did have a future vision of what they wanted for themselves. And they always remembered the importance, the necessity, of profit. Writers and speakers since Napoleon Hill wrote his famous *Think and Grow Rich* have repeated this basic principle. It applies to individuals; it applies to organizations.

The ways in which the company then plans to fulfill its purpose is called a company strategy. Strategy answers the how questions. A business strategy is not simply a business plan. It is not a guarantee for success but without a strategy the odds are much higher that the business will fail. The strategy is the frame work for the larger and more detailed business plan which is more detailed and more apt to change often. It will include particulars about deadlines, reviews, evaluations, staffing requirements, equipment, and all the details of daily operation.

All of these tools serve a valuable purpose. They become a kind of yardstick by which, after a time, the business can measure its progress, evaluate the reality of its goals, and make changes that appear to be necessary. Making those assessments can shed light on how well the company has been managed up to that point. The figures out of the accounting office will tell exactly what has been done. Revisiting strategy and the business plan will show the necessity of a mid-course correction. The two together then form the basis for determining whether to stay the course or begin making necessary changes.

The point here is that focus on the business and the nuts and bolts of making it work takes a lot of thought and represents a lot of work. But, this is what true leaders do. They do not massage numbers or manage earnings in an attempt to boost their stock's price for a day or a quarter. On the contrary, good leaders consider their stocks' prices to be just one part of the whole picture of running their businesses. The managerial focus is where it should be: managing the company and leading the employees to success.

To some managers and CEOs this may all look a little too much like work. It certainly does not have the instant gratification of watching the stock market every day. It is work. After all, though, is that not why we go into business in the first place? If the stock prices increase because the business has been managed to a sound profit, it is a win-win-win situation. The business wins, the customers win, and the shareholders win.

Planning for Profits

It is advisable to review the business strategy once a year at a minimum to see if market conditions have changed, new competition has emerged, or the economy is going through a change. Does the strategy need a facelift? Did the strategy work as well as it was planned to do? This is rightly called taking care of business. It is not taking care of the stock price. Take care of business and the stock price will take care of itself. Take enough time to give this a thorough going over. Everything that comes after will depend on getting this right.

Make sure your business plan is not just a lot of numbers and charts; but at the same time do not write a book that no one will ever read. Make it sharp and concise. If changes in the market, the economy, or the competition have been identified, focus on those and the way your business plan will be altered to meet the new challenges. In other words, do not simply dust off last year's plan and dot a few more i's and cross a few more t's. Look for new goals for the business or, for larger companies, new goals for departments or divisions. Be serious about the matter.

After tackling the strategy and business plan to bring them up to date, it is time to haul out the budget. Resist the common tendency to dust off last year's budget and add 5% here or take away 6% there. That is not budget planning at all. In larger companies, cost reductions should not be across the board cuts. What will happen after the cuts needs to be analyzed carefully. If cuts are needed in R&D that does not necessarily mean the same cuts or percentage of cuts need to be made in the Sales Department. Starting from zero every year is called zero-based budgeting. It is more work, but it is the best way to allocate resources on a continuing basis.

Part of making up the budget is making sales projections. What percent of sales growth is needed for the coming year? That question is often best tackled by committee. Three or four heads are better than one is such a speculative area. You want the sales goal to be stronger than the year before, but at the same time you do not want to set an unrealistic goal. Groups know the market better than any one person. Having a sales manager or, worse, the CEO arbitrarily set the next year's sales goal is futile. Group involvement means group buy-in which in turn means group success more often than not.

> ## "Profit is the reward for serving your customers well."

A major warning in preparing the budget is simply this: Don't just hand it over to the same people who did it last year. What you are going to get is a warmed over version of the old budget. Inject some new blood in the process. It only makes sense that if the guy who worked on the budget last year came out of the R&D department and he had a bias against making any cuts there, the leopard is not going to change its spots. Not even if it can be demonstrated that money was wasted in that area of the budget. This is certainly a time when it is inappropriate simply to look at the bottom line on the new budget. It is not a question of *that* the budget was cut by 5%, but more importantly a question of *where* did we make the cuts?

Another caveat in budgeting is this: remember the customers. How will the budget cuts affect the consumer? If a budget cut saves 6% in some area but results in losing 15% of the customers because they did not like the new product or its packaging, the cut has ended up costing the business much more than it saved.

In making the new budget, more than the bottom line should be taken into consideration. Your business might gross several million dollars more this year than it did in the previous year and your company could be in worse shape than before. Your budget needs to address ways to improve profit margin rather than just profits. In other words, you want to produce more profit from each sales dollar spent. It is very possible for your net profit to go up while your profit margin goes down. This would indicate that you are not as efficient in using your resources to make money. This is bad in the long-run. Net profit margins are just as important as the amount of profit.

Profits and the Customers

The first step to earning profit is not to fixate on the desired profit. Profit is the reward for serving your customers well. The first step is to find out what experience or benefit your customers want, and then to get it to them. The next step is to make sure that the customers are willing to pay you more than your costs. This is the value-added approach. The other approach is to find a way to reduce your costs below what you think the customers are willing to pay. It's your choice. Just remember: most customers are not price driven. If you want to compete on price, then you have to be competitive on costs. There can be only one cheapest product in any market. Try as you will, a competitor can always sell for less than you do. And he will, even if he eventually goes broke.

Now exclude the cheapest competitor from the discussion. All the other competitors are not the cheapest, and only one is the most expensive. Follow along here. This means that the market's buying behavior is based on something other than price. Remember, only one seller is the cheapest. Your task is to find out what that buying factor is. Then and only then can you position your product or service so that your selling price is greater than your cost.

Contented and enthusiastic employees contribute to the profit by increasing sales. They create happy and enthusiastic customers. The idea of a product that sells itself is absurd. If that were true, people would still be driving Edsel's. Cutting employees' perks and accommodations (e.g., the company break room or employee special discounts) are more profit cutting than they are cost cutting. Contented employees tend to produce contented customers. Contented customers equal repeat business that does not require new advertising costs. Turnover in employees is expensive. So is turnover in customers.

Customers want good products at the best possible price. That is true. That is not the only driving factor of the market, however. They also want the best possible service. And what customers really want is a positive total customer experience. They want to feel good about more than your product or service. They want to feel good about doing business with your company.

> **"What customers really want is a positive total customer experience."**

A company's community posture or politics also affects profits. When the CEO of Starbucks announced that he would not supply coffee for our troops in Iraq because he did not support that war, many once loyal customers became ex-customers. As an owner of the company, the CEO is entitled to define his purpose in terms of market segments. It's also a pretty meaningless declaration since the Pentagon procurement office probably wouldn't pay $3.50 per cup of coffee for 160,000 troops. But, his political gesture did more than cost the company some customers. Sensing a Starbucks vulnerability, 7-Eleven and McDonalds began offering specialty coffees in their stores. By insulting some of its customer base, Starbucks opened the door to new competitors in the premium coffee business. On the other hand, community and charitable donations can never make up for a dysfunctional business model. Nor can community good will make up for a financially failing company. Once Enron's problems became public, the Enron sign over the sports stadium in Houston, Texas, disappeared almost overnight.

Taking a SWOT at Business

An important step in making both the budget and the business plan is to take a SWOT at it—examining *strengths, weaknesses, opportunities, threats* that may have a big effect on business in the coming year. There are two reasons for examining the strengths of your company. First, it focuses on the areas where the company is "best." It is important for the entire company to understand these strengths. Second, it allows for time to make sure that the strengths do not slide. Taking strengths for granted is likely to change them into weaknesses. Henry Ford's cheap cars were a strength when he first started churning them out on his assembly lines. His failure to notice that the buying public wanted something different eventually made that strength a weakness.

Weaknesses obviously need to be identified and corrected. If the strength lies in a strong product line but customers are going to the competition, you need to understand why. If it is because, for example, of poor customer service, then concentrating on better products will have limited effect. Beefing up the customer service area of business is called for. More is learned from identifying and correcting weaknesses than from self congratulations on the company's strengths.

Opportunities may come from anywhere, even natural disasters. It is not profiteering to serve people in need. In the aftermath of hurricane Katrina, Wal-Mart got more goods to more people in less time than did FEMA, a government agency established expressly to help people in emergencies. Sometimes opportunities come from government in the form of tax breaks or an easing of regulations. If you find a business for sale that is in your same industry and your company's management has the expertise to operate the acquired business, an acquisition may make good business sense.

Threats to business, likewise, may come from anywhere. Changes in the market are one of the biggest threats. Say your company makes the best darn carbon paper in the world. It will hold up through repeated use and make the clearest carbon copies anyone has ever seen. Suddenly, people start to prefer NCR paper that requires no carbon sheet when they need copies. It makes no difference how good your product is. Now you need to face the threat and make some needed changes. Other threats include new competition in your market area. When Wal-Mart builds a superstore in a new area, some Mom and Pop businesses close their doors. Others, however, do not. They change their purpose and their mission. They find a way to compete in something other than price. In effect, they turn a potential threat into an opportunity.

Wal-Mart is not good in everything. It has weaknesses or areas where it is less strong. Successful competitors have discovered those relative weaknesses. First, they recognized that the greater traffic the superstore would bring into the area could also be their traffic. Next, they changed their advertising focus and increased their accent on customer service. They stressed learning customers by name whenever they came into the store. All employees were taught to refer customers to other stores, including the superstore, when the business did not have exactly what the customers wanted. Through the process of better service, personalization through name recognition, and the willingness to help customers find what they were looking for, these small businesses thrived in the shadows of the big box competition.

Looking for Profit

The fact is that the only reason to go into business is to make a profit. Your purpose is why you went into that particular business. There's an old saying that "profit is not a four-letter word, but loss is." The simple expression that even Junior Achievement students learn is:

Money from sales – Expenses = Profit

Profit may be looked at in terms of absolute dollars. This is usually the approach taken when a critic wants to denigrate a successful company. For example, Exxon in the first quarter of 2007 earned 9.3 billions dollars in net profit. Gee, that sounds like a lot. But, Exxon had to sell 87 billion dollars worth of stuff to make that profit. Exxon also paid more than 6 billion dollars in income taxes. But you won't read about that. Nor will you read that Exxon's profit was only 10.6%. Quite a few other companies make more than 11% profit per year. Exxon's profit margin seems very reasonable for a company that sells high demand products that have functional shortages.

Now consider the alternative. If Exxon had only made one dollar profit last year, but made two dollars profit this year, these same critics would blast the company for increasing its profit 100%. Whenever we have this discussion with otherwise sensible people, we ask the question, "If you were to put $100 in the bank would you want to be paid interest on your money?" The answer is always "yes". Then we ask, "If you deposit another $100 for a total of $200 in your account, would you expect less interest, the same interest, or more interest than when you had $100?" We always get the same answer: everyone wants more interest for having more money on deposit. Exxon's profit is like the interest you would earn on your savings. It is the return on your investment. Exxon should be applauded for selling 87 billion dollars worth of stuff and making 10% profit. In fact, some of the stockholders might sell their Exxon stock if they think another company's stock would earn more than 10%. Just like you might change banks to get a higher rate of interest. The point is this: read the numbers for yourself. You need to know both profit in dollars and profit percentage to tell how your company or any company is doing.

Now consider a company tries to boost stock prices by concentrating on production or sales. When production falls behind during the month, the company may require its employees to work overtime in a concentrated effort to meet the monthly quota of goods produced. The product sells for the same price but the cost of goods sold has just gone up because of overtime so the profit suffers. The monthly quota is met, however, and the stock price is stabilized if not increased. But by the end of the month, the employees are exhausted and for the first week of the next month, production slows again. The last week of the month, then, another push is made to meet the production quota for the next month. The entire cycle begins again. There may be, in any business, a legitimate need for overtime production because of an exceptionally large and unexpected order. Nevertheless, when monthly or quarterly production quotas are benchmarks of the business plan, it is time to step back and reconsider. Was the goal a production quota, or was it profit?

Where Does the Profit Go?

Gross sales are not profit at all. By themselves, sales figures tell you nothing about profit. In fact, there may even be instances when the sales figures are up but the profit is actually down or non-existent. The profit does not all go into the pockets of the owners.

- Corporate income taxes must be paid out of profit.
- Some of the profits must be reinvested in the company
    - building maintenance or expansion
    - possible acquisitions
    - buying equipment
    - perhaps adding additional assembly lines
    - developing new product lines
    - additional employees.

- Profit sharing and pension funds must be paid out of the profits as well. If there are no profits, there can be no pensions.
- The owners of the business (or shareholders) can only be paid out of profits. If there is no profit, there are no dividends. The owners, whether individuals or stockholders, deserve to be paid for investing their money into the business. Moreover, without profits, the owners of the company will quit the business, or the company will go out of business.

It is plain to see, therefore, that even though the money keeps rolling in, there are demands on that money before it reaches the owners. But on a quarterly, monthly, sometimes daily basis, the key to a successful business is not profit but cash flow.

> ***"Profit is the measure of your service to your customers."***

Not only is positive good cash flow happy news to the company, it is also an important factor to those people who want to invest in the company. A positive cash flow statement, not the current price of the company stock, gives investors an idea of how well the company is run. That is why this document is one of the SEC required disclosures. This accounting reveals not only the revenue coming into the company, but it also shows the outflow of cash on business activity.

All large companies today use the accrual method of accounting which includes revenue not actually received. It is possible to show good quarterly results and still have less actual cash than what was available at the beginning of the quarter. Investors look closely to see the cash flow statements as an indication whether or not there is a problem in the company.

Bottom Line is Still the Profit

The point is that a good manager will keep his or her eye on the very basics of business that have been proven since man first put down his plow and started marketing goods or services. Good business management concentrates on marketing a familiar product or service and keeping a vigilant eye on those outside forces that affect the conduct of the business. Management has no control over natural or man-made calamities, but it does have control over how the business reacts to them.

Good business is not about the stock market which is volatile and unpredictable. Repeatedly we have seen how companies that concentrate on stock prices by tweaking the quarterly reports and making splashy announcements in the press have failed. Attention diverted from actually running the company gets shifted toward stock prices and stock options for management. It has resulted in scandal, mismanagement, and the destruction of lives.

Even size is not the answer. Bigger is not always better as many companies have learned the hard way. When bigger only means the additional revenue from an acquired business, it often actually means a lower margin of profit. The American automobile industry as a whole is classic proof of this.

Manage the company by focusing on these business basics. Keep an eye on costs, but not at the expense of customer satisfaction. Customers buy on price if there are no perceived differences between you and your competitors. Give your customers what they want and they will pay your price-a price that lets you cover your costs and make a profit.

Good business is all about profit. It is about finding ways to increase profit regularly. A well-run business will attract its own investors without the need of playing the stock market games where shares are hot today but the company is bankrupt tomorrow.

Profit and loss are the great indicators of the success of a business. Profit is good. Profit is an integral part of your purpose. Profit is the measure of your service to your customers.

Keys to this Chapter

🔑 Profit is not a four-letter word. Loss is.

🔑 Mission statements have been misused to the point that they are worthless.

🔑 It is the owners' responsibility to articulate the company's purpose, mission, and vision.

🔑 If your purpose, mission, and vision truly serve the market, your employees will eagerly help you achieve them.

🔑 But you have to tell your employees what they are.

🔑 Good leaders look at the big picture and the long term. They manage companies, not stock prices.

Chapter Nine

Do What You Know

The cliché, "Keep the main thing, the main thing," has been repeated so many times that Google has over 39 million references to it in the search engine. It may be trite, but there is more than a grain of truth in the idea. It is very much like the standard advice to golfers: "keep your eye on the ball." Losing focus and being inattentive to the core business have caused many companies to founder. At best, the sidetracked executives regret the legitimate opportunities that were overlooked as they dallied in areas beyond their capabilities or expertise. At worst, these companies saw their brands destroyed, customers lost, and sometimes the complete loss of the business. All because those companies and executives forgot why they were in business in the first place.

Rework the Whole Thing

As we discussed before, there are many ways in which companies get off track. One of the major ways is when a CEO becomes enamored with the latest management fad. Re-engineering is a good example. When a crisis looms, the immediate response of many managers is to do something, and to do it quickly. As the saying goes, drastic times call for drastic measures. So the executive decides to change something, even if that something doesn't need changing. The company is struggling so we have to change something. Change is good. Big change is better. Sweeping change is best. Let's bust paradigms, think outside the box, and develop a whole new game plan.

The problem is that most change initiatives are overcorrections. The solution is worse than the original problem. The change can actually end the company. It is the same response young drivers make when their cars drive too close to the edge of the road. These driving novices tend to overcorrect their steering. They turn the opposite way so much that the car is now going too far the other way. If they panic and continue to overcorrect, the car's path oscillates ever more wildly until the car runs off the road and crashes. Some managers run their companies like that.

By making hasty and radical changes in practices, procedures, and personnel these managers tend to overcorrect. They then cause more problems than they started with. As they continue to overcorrect, the company careens from one new paradigm to another, from one fad to another. Nothing is truly solved because the problem was never truly addressed. All the while the employees, the customers, even the shareholders are left watching in disbelief and dismay. At some point the owners effect a change in management, but a lot of damage has been done. Jobs are lost, customers are alienated, and shareholder value has been destroyed. Some good does come of this, however. The managers usually get paid to leave through severance packages that often make them wealthy for the rest of their lives. Very much like paying a dungeon master to stop the tortures.

The fallacy in radical change, the problem with so-called reengineering is this: since the company has been in business for many years, it must have been doing something right. Instead of throwing the company baby out with the bath, a better plan would be to identify what has been working, and then keep doing that. Then, look for what doesn't work, and fix that. Not change for the sake of change, but correction for the sake of correction. Not all change is good.

Management should be looking at the core business. Certain questions should be answered. First, is the product or service still viable in the market? If the product is not obsolete, then the next question might be whether the product is competitive in quality and price. If the answer is positive, management needs to continue looking. A drop in sales does not mean there is a problem with the product. The problem could be in advertising, order fulfillment, delivery times, or company image. Far too often, the immediate reaction to decreasing sales is price reduction. This not only reduces the profit margin from the sales, it fails to address the real underlying problem.

The lesson is to fix what needs fixing. If the core business is down, spin-offs, acquisitions, and joint ventures will do nothing to correct the real problem. Introspection is difficult for individuals; it's difficult for businesses. But good leadership requires that kind of maturity and courage. Owners expect it, and employees deserve it. Chasing the latest fad is not leadership. Making changes to look like you're "engaged" is more than worthless. It is damaging to the organization. Looking closely at all facets of business is an exercise in discovery. Find the chink in the corporate armor. Then fix that defect instead of throwing out the entire suit of armor and making a new one. Chances are that the new suit will have new chinks, maybe even the same old one. Re-engineering has been used far too often to overhaul when a simple tune-up was all that was necessary.

Put on Some Blinders

Maybe the biggest reason management loses sight of its core business is that glamorous word, diversification. It is said that diversification will create synergy, optimize efficiency, decrease duplication, and even out the business cycle. Time and again this approach has proven itself ineffective, yet it persists like the common cold. Diversification's allure lies in the hope that it will cause investors to look favorably on the company (and its management). But diversification has little if anything to do with the basic operation of the company. Diversification not only takes the focus away from the core business, it often distracts management from the most basic model of business.

Basic Business Model

1. Determine what customers want
2. Input raw materials
3. Convert raw materials into finished goods
4. Sell finished goods for more than your costs

Diversification does absolutely nothing to improve the core business or the consumers' satisfaction. In fact, the concept of "core competency" arose as a backlash to the spread of diversification. Diversification is, by definition, the process of acquiring businesses that are outside the core business area. Diversification is almost always a sign that management has failed in its primary mission to grow the core business. As we consultants say, diversification is usually a smokescreen for management's failure to create organic growth.

The illusion caused by diversification often looks good at the outset. The consolidated financial statement shows total revenue much higher than the year before. Sure, there are now two companies instead of one. However, the increased sales came not from selling more stuff to customers. The combined financial statements may even hide an actual decrease in revenue from the original core business which has been neglected in the excitement over the new acquisition. History shows that there is approximately a twenty year cycle where companies diversify and later divest in order to get back to the basics of running the core business.

With attention diverted to diversification and its more complicated management requirements, the core business becomes the forgotten child of the family. But the core business does not run itself. The neglect causes sales to fall and margins to disappear. General Motors is probably the biggest example we have. At one time General Motors was not only the largest automaker in the United States, it sold almost as many cars as all the other manufacturers combined. Over the years GM made two major management blunders. First, it ignored consumers' changing tastes and second, it tried to buy labor peace through extravagant wage and benefit concessions. As margins shrank and black ink turned to red, GM bought other car companies instead of addressing its core business and its core problems. GM tried to buy growth in other companies instead of creating growth internally. Its acquisitions were really superficial solutions to deeper problems.

Plan it to Death

Strategic planning is a valuable management tool. Unfortunately, its application swings between seldom and constant. Mostly, strategic planning is talked about, but rarely practiced. Managers are too busy with day to day operations-and their problems-to give much thought to strategy. On the flip side, strategic planning becomes another fad when the CEO gets the strategy religion and mandates forecasts, meetings, and plans in an attempt to create the perfect plan or perhaps, to know the unknowable. Citicorp is typical. In most years, strategic planning was put on the shelf. There were companies to buy, resources to redeploy, new markets to penetrate. As earnings started to stagnate, shareholders started to ask, how big is too big? What is the purpose of all this? (There's that purpose thing again). All of a sudden, management goes on a strategic planning tear. This is when strategic planning can actually be counterproductive. The damage is done when strategic planning becomes a monster that weights down division and department heads under an avalanche of unnecessary paperwork. During the time that all that "planning" is being done, the core business is left alone to operate as it has been. Nobody is really "flying the plane" in the false anticipation that all problems will be miraculously solved once the strategic plans are written down. Offices the world over contain shelves of useless plans and manuals that have never been opened since the day they were printed. A strategic plan should not take on the proportions of compiling an encyclopedia. If the plan is centered on the primal reasons for being in business in the first place, a strategic plan will simply address four things:

1. What is our current situation? What are our resources and values? Our strengths and weaknesses? What does the competitive landscape look like?

2. What is our vision? What are we trying to achieve and what will our preferred future look like?

3. What actions will we take that take advantage of our strengths and minimize the obstacles to our success?

4. Can we summarize these actions into a general plan that we will follow regardless of temporary setbacks? Can we use the plan as an overall guide to help us accomplish our mission and achieve our vision?

It should be noted that doing what a company knows best doesn't mean staying stuck in time. Following your core competency also means keeping up with change. Nothing stays the same. Rapid change is nowhere as obvious as in the electronics sector. For example, when postage meters became obsolete because of new technology, Pitney Bowes did not simply continue manufacturing the same machines. Their core competency was in bulk mail handling, not in the manufacturing of specific machines. What they knew and understood was how to handle large volumes of mail quickly and inexpensively. Applying that competency to the changes taking place in the bulk mail industry, Pitney Bowes developed the hardware and software to make bulk mail handling easier. The company maintained its leadership in the market by adapting to change within its own area of expertise.

> *"Diversification is usually a smokescreen for management's failure to create organic growth."*

As a business consultant and an expert on growing businesses, I have worked with both companies and entrepreneurs who said they wanted to grow their businesses. What they really wanted was more income. Typically, the story goes like this: the owner or CEO complains that business is slow. The reason given is usually something that is said to be beyond the control of the owner/executive. The words are almost identical every time: "This is a tough business. Everybody knows you can't make money in this business". And this is from multi-million dollar corporations and highly compensated professionals. In the case of individuals, they told me about starting supplemental businesses because they were not satisfied with their primary incomes. When they tried moonlighting or sideline businesses, however, these people met with failure because their primary occupations prevented them from putting in the 100% effort necessary to make the second business successful. The new ventures also become distractions from day jobs, thus diverting energy, time, and resources which might have been better spent on primary careers. Companies are no different. Too many managers get frustrated when their companies suffer from slow growth or no growth. But instead of fixing the problem, instead of building on strength to grow the business from the inside, these executives look to outside businesses for sales and earnings growth. In that respect, the merger and acquisition trend is no different than the professional who moonlights to make some extra money.

My advice has always been the same to those individuals or businesses. Put all your time, energy, and resources into your primary career or product, the areas where you already have expertise. This is where your experience, your industry knowledge, your contacts, and your customers are. The return on investment on your core business is potentially so much greater than any other venture or endeavor.

If sales in your core business are not increasing, find out why. You may discover that you simply need to improve the product quality, add more models to the line, add features the customers want, or extend the brand. In simple terms, expand and improve your line of *gizmos* before you consider adding *widgets*. Concentrate on being the master of *gizmos* and have better gizmos than anyone else.

Some Current Winners

Looking over the Forbes 200 of best small companies (sales of $5 million to $750 million) there is strong evidence to support the idea that companies succeed when they "do what they know." Many of these companies took their specialized knowledge into new or niche markets and recorded phenomenal growth in 2006 over the previous year. Here is a brief recap on some of the top 10:

- **NutriSystems, Inc.**—Number one on the Forbes list, this company is a textbook example of how to succeed by concentrating on the core business. It was not always so. According to David Whelan of Forbes, the company, founded in 1971 by Harold Katz, entered the market as a product-based competitor to Weight Watchers. It started off with a liquid protein drink that was a hot product in the 70's until some crash dieters using the product developed fatal heart problems. Shape Up, as the company was called back then, changed its name to NutriSystem Foods of the Future 2000 and transitioned into marketing food for the diet conscious. The company went public in 1981. Right away, the company acquired the Philadelphia 76ers basketball team, bought a company jet, and built new headquarters. A change in ownership resulted in the selling off of assets, but this failed to revive the ailing company. In addition, billboard ads across the country claimed that the company's food was overpriced and caused painful gallstones. Despite a successful lawsuit for defamation, the Nutrisystem brand was badly hurt. After going into Chapter 11 bankruptcy, the company was bought by a Chicago billionaire who introduced an herbal mixture that was later banned by the FDA. He also implemented an unsuccessful Mary Kay-like marketing program and built a number of "wellness centers." None of these steps was effective. The company was still deeply troubled.

  Then Michael Hagan stepped in and imposed a back-to-basics strategy. As soon as Hagan took over, he put the weight loss company on its own diet. He sold assets and businesses that were not aligned with the purpose and mission of the company. Hagan cut out all the middlemen such as wholesalers, distributors, and retailers to concentrate on the core business: marketing reduced calorie meals directly to weight conscious consumers. In the last five years, revenue has jumped from $28 million to $413 million dollars. Profit has ballooned from $2 million to $55 million. None of this came from diversification. It is the result of the company doing what it does best.

- **Hansen Natural**—this company, specializing in natural flavor fruit drinks and popular energy drinks, started out as a small, local company in Southern California. Its main customers at that time were Hollywood studios. Over the years it has grown steadily, always centered on it core business. Its acquisitions have all been other drink companies or a few complementary snack related companies. By remaining fixed on its area of expertise, Hansen Natural's growth earns it a number two rank on the *Forbes* list.

- **optionsXpress**—a leader in online stock trading (at number 3 on the *Forbes* list), it is another company with its eyes fixed on its core competency. For the past five years, optionsXpress has been rated as best online brokerage by *Forbes, Barron's, Kiplinger's and Smart Money.* Their program is based on three E's—**educating** customers about options, teaching how to **evaluate** their options, and **executing** customers' decisions quickly and reasonably priced. Their company motto just about sums it up: "Potential is Interesting; Performance is Everything."

- **PetMed Express**—a relative newcomer in the business world, PetMed Express is a clear example of persistence in the face of odds against success. The whole idea of core business is one of constantly looking for ways to make it work or work better. PetMed's business is providing veterinary medicine directly to pet owners via the internet. In order to do business it had to ward off challenges by veterinary groups which feared it would interfere with their businesses. Then it had to gain the cooperation of pharmaceutical companies that did not want to alienate the veterinarians.   By keeping focused on its product and service, PetMed managed to overcome those obstacles. Here is a great example of not looking for external, unrelated answers in business.   No fad business model could possibly have accomplished what PetMed did by concentrating all its energy, time, and resources into making the company work.

Looking Beneath the Surface

Evidence indicates that knee jerk solutions to indications that a company is facing trouble are almost always wrong. Circuit City is undoubtedly learning that lesson the hard way. To the general public, let alone business advisors, their massive firings of what they considered "over-paid" employees was viewed as an insult. People sympathized with the fired employees. More than that, they resented the message sent to the customers. That message told customers that they had no right to expect expert assistance when shopping at Circuit City. Shoppers were told that low salaried new employees were all that they deserved.

Circuit City failed to consider its core competency in making the decision to fire its top employees.   The company is not a manufacturer. Its competency has always been bringing together a wide selection of electronic products to sell under one roof. Circuit City's objective was actually to offer a wide range of consumer technology items, to educate their customers on the technology, and to help the customers buy the products that best suit their needs. This formula helped the company grow as technology increased faster than customers could keep up. Customers became accustomed to talking to knowledgeable employees who had the expertise to guide them toward the products which satisfied their needs. By firing those employees, the company literally abandoned two of the three keys to its competitive strategy. Recently, there has been talk within the company of reducing the breadth of product offerings in the stores. This, of course, eliminates the last of the three key elements to its previous success. If the company continues down this path, it's difficult to see how they can compete in any area except price. Historically, the companies that compete on price- especially in the tech markets-increasingly struggle until they fail.

Experienced personnel are an important part of any company's core competency. Letting those people go and replacing them with lower paid workers was short-sighted and counterproductive. To look seriously at the core business, everything that goes into making it successful needs to be carefully examined. The widget manufacturer needs those people who are experts in widgets and contribute toward making them distinctive. A struggling company really needs its best people to stay on and help effect the turnaround. If the sale of widgets has declined, firing the experts is likely not getting to the root of the problem. Examined closely, widget management may discover the real reason for the decline lies more in management's resistance to changing market conditions.

Western Auto was a company formed in 1909 just as the American automotive industry started to take off. These stores became synonymous with automobile service and parts for do-it-yourself car repairs. The company brand extended to the moderately priced Western Flyer bicycle that enabled thousand of kids to enjoy two-wheel transportation. Its service centers provided the bulk of its profits enabling the company to sell auto parts at competitive prices. In small town America, the name Western Auto was synonymous with quality and service.

In 1987, Sears bought a majority interest in the company. Sears then increased Western Auto's tire selections, added Craftsman tools to its inventory, and pushed the sale of Sears' Die Hard batteries. The service part of Western Auto's business was deemphasized and gradually phased out. As the company continued to wither, Sears sold its Western Auto holdings only eleven years after acquiring them. The company was then acquired by Advance Auto Parts. The repair facilities are long gone, but the low cost auto parts that had been the core of Western Auto's business were once again the central focus. Only now, the name on the sign is Advance. The original Western Auto is just another entry in the list of companies that lost their way.

Another great example of a business that started well, ran successfully for many years, but failed to keep up with the times is S. S. Kresge stores. Mr. Kresge could arguably be called the father of the "five and dime" store. The stores were icons of Middle America for over four decades. Then, during the Second World War, Kresge saw another business opportunity and opened stores where everything sold for less than a dollar. His innovations in retailing became the inspiration for the big box discount stores that came later. In 1977, S. S. Kresge stores became K-Marts and should have owned the low-cost retail segment. But, K-Mart lost its Middle America focus and was soon overtaken by a discount chain from Arkansas called Wal-Mart.

As mentioned earlier, Bill Greehey was cited as a stark contrast to the celebrity CEO. Leader of Valero Energy Company from its beginnings in 1980, Greehey kept his eyes on the core business of supplying energy. In the process of its phenomenal growth over the past two decades, Valero has only made acquisitions that were within the expertise of the Valero management. The acquisitions were made also when a smaller company owned a process that would be useful across the board for the parent company. Greehey also placed great emphasis on the employees of Valero, even considering himself in that category. By keeping focused on the core business, making changes as needed through the years, and operating at a high level of ethics, Valero grew from a beginning company into a top performer among the Fortune 500.

By contrast, a company that seems to have lost its edge is Motorola. The rise to a position of dominance for Motorola came as the company registered more patents than any other company in the electronics business. From its earliest years, Motorola emphasized research and development. The company was actively "inventing" new products at the rate of one or two per year. At one time, its cellular flip phones were considered the cutting edge of style. In fact, Motorola pioneered the development of quality radios for automobiles (hence the name Motorola). Ironically, the company is no longer in the car radio business even though its expertise paved the way for onboard navigation systems like OnStar. Today, instead of developing new patents, the company has been acquiring them through acquisitions. In the meantime,

Nokia has used the early Motorola model of providing reasonably priced and innovative equipment to dominate the world market for cell phones. Also, as a result of its reduced emphasis on R&D, Motorola was slow to make the transition from analogue to digital telephony. Somewhere along the line, the management of Motorola mistook its core business which was convenient and reliable personal communications, and not a specific phone technology.

The Area of Expertise

It's always amazing that managers seem to think they can buy their way out of trouble by buying another company. Where is the logic in assuming that a company can manage an acquisition well when it cannot manage its own business? If the profit margins are stagnant the answer is find the problem and fix it. That comes from hard analysis and diligent work. There are no magic bullets. It is unlikely that taking on the responsibility of managing another company is going to make the parent company run better. And rarely is the acquiring management team the best choice to run the acquired company. Yet thousands of companies go through this silliness every year only to have the mergers come undone a few years later.

The core competencies within any business generally hold the key to revitalizing that business. There may be many areas in which the company can build on what is already in place. Instead of looking outward for solutions, the best place to start is right at home. There are several considerations that provide clues as to how to proceed:

- What is it about our product or service that we can do better than anyone else? Maybe the quality of the product or service is the best in the industry. Maybe the delivery of the product is the best in the business. Pinpoint what the company does best.
- Is the pricing structure right? An interesting study on buyer perceptions recently discovered that when products which had superior features were priced approximately equal to plain products, the feature rich products were perceived to be inferior in quality. When the price is

proportional to the features and utility, the quality is perceived to be higher. Just an example of a pricing structure that may wrong.

- Are key personnel being utilized to maximum productivity? Instead of laying off experienced people on the doubtful grounds that they are overpaid, it might be a wise decision to place those people where they can train more inexperienced employees and/or have more contact with the customers.

- Could sales and profits be enhanced by entering into working partnerships to outsource certain of the company's non-core but necessary functions? Some business functions may be handled more efficiently by outside organizations geared to deal with those functions.

- Is there a weakness in our sales efforts? Even good products do not sell themselves. A close look at the company's marketing plan may offer opportunity for improvement.

- Is the product or service of the company keeping up with current developments? The horse collar factories that switched to making leather car seats survived. Those that kept on making horse collars disappeared.

- Have we really been listening to the consumers? If sales that once were brisk have suddenly gone flat, the customer is telling the company something. That something might range from needed product improvements to problems in customer service.

- What did the company do right in the past that is not working today? There is likely a big clue in answering this question. Most likely, there has been a shift away from concentrating on the core business somewhere down the line.

The purpose of an exercise like the above is to zero in on the problem. First it is necessary to locate the problem before doing the necessary overhaul. When you take the family automobile in for a minor problem, you don't want the mechanic to start repairs until he has a good idea of what is wrong. Ironically, though, businesses often fall into the habit of rushing to find a fix when they do not even know what the exact problem might be.

Let us consider a hypothetical business situation. The XYZ Widget Company has been in business for fifteen years. From the very first year of operation it grew steadily. Revenues were up every year and by carefully controlling costs, the profit margins improved annually as well. Then about two years ago, revenues began to level out. It didn't seem to be a change in the industry because the competition seemed to be doing well.

> **"Do what you know and work toward doing it better than anyone else."**

One executive saw an opportunity to buy out ABD Sprocket Company and convinced the board that this was the answer. Revenues would surely double the next year. And, indeed, they did. The increase, however, was not from increases in the core business but simply from the added revenues generated by ABC. Over the next five years, neither the XYZ Company nor the ABC Company actually grew. The increased revenues that first year did not reflect an increase in profit margin. It was just an increase from combining companies.

On the other hand, if the management of XYZ Company sat down to take a good look at its core business rather than seeking to increase revenues through acquisition, the result would have been much better. Suppose XYZ management locates the problems that are causing sales and revenue to stagnate and sets about to correct them. By addressing the true problem and not trying to cover weak sales with acquisitions, sales and profits will increase in real terms.

Yesterday's success does not ensure success today or tomorrow. What works today will most likely not work tomorrow. Changes in production and distribution are continuous. We've come to expect almost daily changes in electronics and technology but tend to overlook their influence in other industries. Even in children's toys, change and innovation are necessities. The top selling doll of yesterday is obsolete unless it can now talk, walk, and recognize spoken commands. But these changes do not change a company's core business, be it personal communications, mailing systems, or toys. This is why core competency, like a company's purpose and mission can not be product based.

The best path to success is to stay focused on the company's core business, and not get distracted by fads, merger mania, or tomorrow's stock price. Your core business is where your strength and expertise lay. This is where you are most competitive. Pitney Bowes stopped making hand operated postage meters but remembered that its expertise was in the larger business of bulk mail handling. Valero went from being just a petrochemical distributor to becoming a major refiner. Yamaha Corporation began as an organ manufacturer. Today it is the largest manufacturer of musical instruments in the world. All of them grew by concentrating on their core strengths and expertise.

Yamaha Motor Corporation might seem to be an exception to this strategy. After all, this subsidiary of Yamaha Corporation makes engines for recreational vehicles such as motorcycles, snowmobiles, and golf carts. But a closer look reveals that the motor division was set up as a separate entity with separate management. The instrument people let the engine people do what they do best. Warren Buffett doesn't produce anything directly. He just buys companies. It is a pure investment model driven by acquiring companies. But as Buffett himself admits, much of his success comes from buying good companies and then leaving management alone to run their businesses.

Nokia Corporation entered a business area that had been dominated for decades by Motorola. By staying focused on its core business and investing heavily in R&D, Nokia has become the world's leader in cell phone technology and manufacturing. Nokia's success has resulted from the constant effort to keep up with fickle customer demands as well as the long-term innovation that keeps it a technological leader in its industry.

The lesson from these successful companies is clear. Do what you know and work toward doing it better than anyone else. Keep up with changing customer preferences while anticipating future trends. Invest in technological improvements that will improve the products, services, or the way you do business. Constantly working to develop the core business is hands down the best approach.

Keys to this Chapter

🔑 Do what you know. Rarely is your primary market saturated or your market share maximized.

🔑 Strategic plans get talked about a lot, but seldom articulated, and even less often implemented.

🔑 The problem with management fads is that they distract the company from its core business. The fad becomes the business.

🔑 One problem with mergers/acquisitions: if you can't run your own company successfully, how do you expect to run someone else's company successfully?

🔑 Another problem with mergers/acquisitions: the acquisition masks the problems in the parent company. Instead of buying another company's sales and profits, your time would be better spent working on your company's sales and profits.

🔑 Growth is good. Change is necessary. But keeping up doesn't necessarily mean branching out. Stick with what you know. Make it better. Be the best.

Chapter Ten

You Can't Cut Your Way to Prosperity

Maybe this describes your situation: problems loom and seem to get worse with every passing day. Your company is operating inefficiently; there are too many employees for the amount of work to be done. Many managers would simply reduce staff. But now that you've read this far, isn't it obvious that reducing the workforce is completely backwards? The problem is not too many employees; the problem is not enough work to keep them busy. They used to be busy or else you wouldn't have hired them in the first place. So what went wrong? Management went wrong. It's up to management to fix it. Better management in the first place would have avoided this situation.

For our purposes, we'll call it sloppy management when the company is inefficient, disorganized, and distracted. Slack management occurs when the company misses markets, fails to heed changing customer preferences, or misses changes in the economy that can adversely affect the company. Both represent management failure. When confronted with either type of managerial deficiency, a manager will quite often scratch his head, clueless as to what he should do. In a panic, the manager grasps at anything that he thinks might help him out of his dilemma.

According to Leadership IQ, failed change efforts or just plain failure to change is the number one reason that managers are fired. It doesn't really matter whether the problem is slack management or sloppy management. Failure to change can mean failure to keep up with market changes. But, it can also mean failure to take appropriate corrective action when necessary. Usually those failed efforts involve cutting costs, including staff. The thinking is that if costs can be cut significantly, the business will show a profit. If we pare back our operation (downsizing), our costs will go down and the business will begin to show a profit.

The problem with this kind of reasoning is that it pays no attention to repairing the broken business model. The problem is often compounded by the fact that the players who could have been key to turning around the company might have been ushered out the door in employee reductions. Just downsizing without fixing the dysfunctional business model and faulty processes can be the death knell of an already dying company. You can't shrink your way to prosperity. Downsizing can actually *cause* the failure of a company that could have been fixed. To both investors and customers alike, downsizing may come across as a last gasp for survival. No one wants to invest in a company that clearly cannot run its own business. Customers do not want to buy products that may be dinosaurs in the near future.

> **"You can't shrink your way to prosperity."**

Trimming away at a failing company, however, is most often the first step management takes to reverse company fortunes.

Then Why Do They Do It?

Under astute management, downsizing may actually be a viable way of bringing the company back into prosperity. If the downsizing is done for the right reason and in the right way, it can be successful. Investors and customers alike may respond favorably to the news. However, it is a move that bears close scrutiny. If no discernable results are seen within a reasonable time after the downsizing, the shrunken company is left worse than it was before.

The CEO who resorts to downsizing (to fix a problem he or she caused in the first place) often looks at first like a hero. He gets good press and the stock prices may rise for a short time. The bankers look at the situation favorably believing that the business will be able to handle its debts. In fact, downsizing can temporarily mitigate a cash flow problem. It still has not, however, addressed the reason cash flow went south. For a while it looks like a solution, but a downsized company still operating under a dysfunctional business model remains in a precarious situation.

The Turnaround Model

In our consulting business, we have had the opportunity to work with a number of companies that were struggling and facing bankruptcy. We developed a simple model for turnaround management that we used to explain the process to creditors, suppliers, employees, and even the CEO/owner!

1. Do whatever it takes to convert negative cash flow to positive cash flow. This can include staff cuts, but our preferred model is to renegotiate debt payments, work out forbearance with suppliers, and work with anyone who can help convert assets to cash. If employees are the most important asset-as most companies profess-then staff cuts should be last on the list.

2. Now that cash flow is positive, we take a hard look at what went wrong. What happened to the company to cause the lack of profit and negative cash flow? There is something intrinsically wrong with the current business model. Negative cash flow is not the real problem. It is just a symptom.

3. We develop a new business plan and model that addresses the previous problems. This eventually may mean new products, new markets, new customers, but definitely a

change in the way the company does business. The old way didn't work.

4. We implement the new model. When the new model proves it can crank out profit, even with the downsized company, we now have a workable business model.

5. We use this model to grow the company because we know it works. If it works on a smaller scale, it can work on a larger scale.

Some Positives to Downsizing

- As already mentioned, downsizing may result in an improved and positive cash flow. So long as incoming revenues decrease less than the decrease in costs, cutting costs will result in more cash to the company. That does not mean that the company is improving or growing, however. The likelihood is that reducing costs will reduce revenues by the same amount or more. Reducing inventory costs, for example, may result in higher unit costs, higher shipping costs, and lost sales from lack of product. Reducing payroll may cause remaining employees to work overtime. This negates much of the payroll savings. It is also doubtful that the workforce can work overtime for a significant length of time. So, the improved cash flow is just a temporary fix. Its benefit is buying the company time to work on the real problems within the business.

- The resulting improved cash flow may enable the business to avoid breach of loan covenants. In fact, positive cash flow can help the company access additional credit. It also indicates that the company is current with all creditors. Turning negative cash flow to positive is called the crisis mode in turnaround management.

- Along with the positive cash flow, downsizing may induce lenders to extend more credit. Initially, downsizing a company can be looked at favorably by lenders. But, selling off assets is no more a successful business model than is jettisoning cargo from a leaking ship. Success is more than positive cash flow. Eventually, the company must prove that it can generate profit.

- Downsizing may be effective in eliminating overcapacity as well as overstaffing. Overcapacity occurs when ability to supply exceeds demand. There may have been valid reasons for adding capacity in the past. When changes occur in the market or the economy or competition enters the market with something radically new, there may still be a demand for the company's products, but the larger capacity now exceeds reasonable projections for demand. Overcapacity also includes overstaffing, but that is not the only way overstaffing occurs. Sloppy management often happens during boom times when hiring gets all out of control and every request for more personnel is granted. With the downsized company, production capacity is reduced, possibly even selling off assets that are no longer needed. Fewer staff are then needed to produce the products or services. The relevant question is: how did the company get overstaffed?

- Downsizing may be the only option at some point. If the choices are downsizing or go out of business, the better choice is to perform radical surgery but keep the patient alive. Laying off some employees is better than closing the plant altogether.

- Perhaps the most positive effect of downsizing is the resulting forced operational and fiscal discipline that was lacking before. This will not necessarily happen automatically and should be a major purpose of the restructuring in the first place. The operational discipline needed may require more work to be done by fewer people who may have been demoralized by the downsizing. The fiscal discipline will involve cutting out unnecessary spending and identifying and utilizing cost cutting methods. It almost always means a change in the way the company is run.

- In many cases the need to downsize results in a wake-up call for both management and employees. If management does some serious soul searching during the downsizing, the management mistakes of the past need not be repeated. The employees get the message that layoffs were necessary, but are completed. After the initial shock of the restructure wears off, dread may turn into industry as management and employees get down to the serious business of running the company.

- Saving the company and thereby saving their own jobs can be a strong motivation for the remaining employees in a downsized company. Reviving that kind of motivation needs to come from the top. Management needs to show that everyone in the company is called on to put in extra effort. This is unlikely to happen, however, if the layoffs have occurred while managers received bonuses.

The lesson here is that downsizing because of external, uncontrollable factors may have positive results. It is a case of doing the right thing for the right reason. Communicated clearly to employees, all cards on the table, it can repurpose and reenergize a complacent organization. In other words, employees see the need for change because of the situation, not because a manager said so. The main thing is to honestly address the circumstances that caused the need for the downsizing. Management needs to adopt Harry Truman's *The Buck Stops Here* motto and take responsibility for management missteps. Even if externals caused the business to stagnate or decline, management should acknowledge its role in the problem.

The business must now have a new vision that puts the recent difficulties in the past. When the mistakes have been identified, the new rallying point is avoiding those mistakes in the future. Only management can assure the employees in the aftermath of a downsizing. Management should be able to lay out clearly the direction of the smaller company and be able to give reasonable assurances that such measures will not happen again. In other words, the actual downsizing is not the end; it is the beginning.

It is up to management to inject new life into the company after the downsizing. To really be effective, the reformed company must demonstrate a new energy from the top down. If management is enthusiastic about the future, employees will be enthusiastic. The resulting opportunities may include better marketing, or new products or services that can be developed now that the cash flow situation is stabilized. It may mean new opportunities for job advancement in the reorganized company. Most importantly, management can promote the idea that everyone is in this together.

> *"A large company with a flawed business model that is downsized only produces a smaller company with a flawed business model."*

The "Downs" of Downsizing

Lest we paint too rosy a picture of downsizing, let's consider the many negative results of downsizing a company. Successful companies do not need downsizing. Downsizing means a company is in trouble. There are so many steps a company can take to find and correct problems. We consider downsizing a last resort toward making a company work. Unfortunately, executives seem all too eager to trim their companies rather than fix the real problems. Most likely, this is because making companies work takes work. Downsizing is the quick fix that causes stock analysts to cheer and stock prices to surge. In the long run, however, there are many repercussions that usually follow a company downsizing.

- Downsizing means that some people will be leaving. Call it a layoff, a reduction in force, or whatever fancy euphemism you want to put on it, people are getting pink slips—most often with little advance warning. The emotions of loss or anger that run through the people being fired will also run through the minds of the employees who stay. Morale hits a low that many times cannot be reversed. Such feelings cannot always be mitigated by managers even though they profess concern for the employees who are leaving by providing counseling and job search assistance. The worst case scenario occurs when management adopts an attitude of, "Don't let the door hit you as you leave."

Poor morale leads to poor performance which leads to poor customer service which leads to more lost business. The remaining employees quickly develop an indifferent attitude toward their work and the company in general. "If they did that to people I worked with for years, what's to keep them from doing it to me?" is the thought on the minds of the remaining employees.

- Downsizing correctly requires a surgeon and not a butcher. Typically, managers make cuts in the wrong places. If management has not clearly identified the areas that need the surgery, there is a danger of cutting a vital organ-an area that will cause further damage to the company. A common mistake made during downsizing is telling each department to cut a certain percentage for an across-the-board reduction.

- When the cuts are made to downsize, there is a danger that the cuts may be too deep and ultimately cause operations to suffer. Reducing the size of an operation requires great skill and forethought. Nothing has been accomplished by selling off space, for example, that is needed for production. Nothing has been accomplished either when too many jobs have been cut only to discover that the remaining workforce cannot meet quotas and deadlines. Today, using the 1950's model of reducing headcount is risky business. Considering the expanding global markets, deep cuts may result in lacking the experienced talent that is needed to take advantage of opportunities. In that case if new employees need to be hired, that further demoralizes the workforce. It shows a lack of adequate planning and destroys employees' (and customers') confidence in the management of the company. Refer back to the dubious decision of Circuit City to fire "overpaid employees" which was perceived by many customers as an indifference to good customer service.

- As a rule, downsizing is a motivator. It motivates the best people in a company to start looking for other jobs. They may have been happy to stay with the company before. Now, their fear of being next in the unemployment lines causes them to update their resumes. Once they are open to leaving, they have no problem finding new jobs simply because they *are* the best. The ones who remain are the least valuable people in the organization. Investors and customers alike become aware of the departures, and confidence in the company wanes. The type of downsizing that is often referred to as "outsourcing" may have the same effect on the best employees. There is also the possibility that the outsourced workers are less capable than the ones now lost forever to the company. If the outsourcing doesn't work as well as planned, there is no good way to bring the work back in-house. The people who used to do that work are gone.

- Most important of all is the fact that downsizing does not address the original problem. It is a kind of bandage that can only offer temporary relief. In most cases, if the real problem is identified and work begins immediately to fix the real problem, downsizing become unnecessary. Unless the problem has been caused by economic changes in the market or some catastrophic event, identifying the real problem and fixing it is almost always the best approach.

In my observations as a consultant, CEOs who are quick to downsize are usually trying to gloss over their own managerial mistakes and weaknesses. On paper, the idea of downsizing looks like a brilliant solution to a cash flow problem. Boards and investors are encouraged…at first. But management's responsibility is to work for the long-term, sustainable success of the company, not go for the quick fix or the fad solution. That's why owners hire managers. That's why shareholders invest money. Neither wants to run the company. They want to make money now and in the future.

Ironically, it is possible that the temporarily improved cash flow in the business may actually exacerbate the problem. Creating better cash flow without addressing the real problem only provides more cash to keep on doing the wrong things.

- It should be patently clear by now that downsizing is a flawed business model that only produces a smaller version of the flawed business model. This is the obvious result when downsizing is viewed as an end in itself. Shrinking the size of a company is a matter of scale rather than a matter of management. While it may improve the cash flow problems for a time, it does not address the flaws that caused it to be necessary in the first place. At the risk of sounding redundant, a large company with a flawed business model that is downsized only produces a smaller company with a flawed business model. It is like a bully who goes on a diet. The diet does not change the bully's behavior. It only produces a smaller bully.

- Finally, one of the dangers of downsizing is the tendency for history to repeat itself. Many CEOs see the improved cash flow and begin at once wanting to re-grow the company. Using the same flawed business model, the results are predictable—another dysfunctional company. The history of business practices in America is replete with examples of what can only be classified as mismanagement. The chemical companies in the 1980s are good examples as they all, it seems, rushed to diversify and later found that their management was not capable of directing the newly acquired businesses.

The resulting divestitures that followed in the 1990's brought about tens of thousands of job losses. As in the case when Eastman Kodak backed away from pharmaceuticals by selling off to Elf Sanofi, it became clear that the buying company had little or no interest in the buildings or the personnel. Their purchase was because of an interest in owning existing products and the rights to a few others that were not yet being marketed. Suddenly chemists were out beating the bushes for employment.

Downsizing and restructuring also hit major companies like DuPont and Mobil Chemical resulting in thousands of layoffs for chemists. The human costs and destruction of morale for those who did not get cut were devastating. Perhaps the only good thing that came out of such massive layoffs was that those affected were not stigmatized because of the vast number of layoffs that had occurred. The saddest thing about the layoffs was that after two years, 70% of the companies involved realized that the downsizings had accomplished nothing.

There are Keys to Long-Term Success

"Haste makes waste" can certainly be applied to the sudden urge to downsize for improved cash flow. Identifying and correcting the real problems are the only ways to repair a flawed business model. These are the steps that must be taken to make this happen:

1. There is a problem. It is easy to see that the business is not performing well. Therefore, the very first step is one of analysis. This requires the time to search out the root cause or causes of the downturn. The real problem is seldom as simple as overstaffing. Something in the system is not working and it must be identified. Unless this analysis is done and clearly understood, trying to implement solutions is an exercise in futility. It resembles the late Johnny Carson's Karnack the Magnificent, attempting to give answers when he did not know what the questions were. For Karnack, the answers resulted in high comedy; for businesses, putting the solution before the problem results in disaster.

2. Once the problem or problems have been clearly identified, the correct response is to fix those problems. Compare it to a man who runs out to buy a smaller car because his big car drove into a ditch. The smaller car might get better gas

mileage and thus improve the man's cash flow, but it will not prevent the smaller car from driving into the same ditch. The answer is to fix the real problem which is the man's inability to keep his car on the road.

3. In those cases where downsizing is absolutely necessary to remedy a situation or alleviate a crisis, it must be done quickly and decisively. Repeated rounds of downsizing or repeated layoffs are deadly to a business. It clearly demonstrates to everyone—employees, customers, and investors—that management is indecisive, incompetent, or both.

4. Once the downsizing has been accomplished, the immediate need is the creation of a viable and PROFITABLE business model at the new, smaller sized company. Downsizing is not the answer to business difficulties. It is a tool to save a faltering company. It is a first step at best. Now attention must be turned to the core competencies in the smaller business to design a new business model. It is essential that the mess created by the restructure be cleaned up immediately. The time bought by the restructuring sometimes eliminates the urgency to do the difficult task of fixing the true problems. If the downsizing was done properly, there may be time to get smarter while costs are lowered and cash flow is improved. Sensible outsourcing of non-critical operations might solve a workforce problem. Whatever the problem was in the past, it is vital that the same mistakes not be allowed to repeat themselves.

5. Good management will resist the rush to expand as the cash flow situation increases. The goal is to double the business and therefore doubling the profits while maintaining the margins or even improving on them. Only when this kind of growth has been accomplished is it time to consider expansion. Doubling the size of a company is not the same thing as doubling the profits. Adding stores, going nationwide, or globalizing are only viable after the company is positioned and ready for growth. A rush to

expand as soon as the revenues start to increase is a recipe for making the same mistakes that caused the original problems.

6. Carving out a solid, workable model at one location is the best advice. As the model is being tested, it can be tweaked from time to time as needed. Then the model can be scaled for expansion. Proving a new model on a small scale reduces the risks of restructuring. It is a way to guard against making catastrophic mistakes on a large scale like what happened before.

7. The common denominator to any restructuring, any downsizing, is change. If you keep doing what you've always done, you'll keep getting what you've always gotten. The company will simply have to change the way it does business. But most people are greatly resistant to change. According to Leadership IQ, most managers avoid change, change too slowly, or fail in their attempts to impose meaningful change. The resistance to change on the part of management is one of the underlying causes of business failures in the first place. Just as it is management's responsibility to lead the company in good times, it is also management's responsibility to lead the company through change, especially painful change.

   a. To be sure, change is difficult. It requires a new way of thinking and new ways of doing things. Recognizing that changes are necessary is not the problem that implementing those changes creates. Management must be the leader in making changes. Management must set the example and communicate the need for change effectively. When the failure to change is the real problem with the company, then it becomes clear that more flexible management, or managers, are called for.

8. In the process of making the needed changes once the problem has been identified, there are some major factors to include in the planning process:

9. Identify the key players that will be involved in the restructuring. Change involves people, their willingness to change, and their ability to change. The process may involve training that might be called re-skilling.

10. Write out in plain language exactly what the changes are and the expected results of the changes. This is not the time to be vague. This process may prove to be a bit painful because it implies faulty management and operations in the past.

11. Be sure to check out all the governmental and environmental legalities that might affect the change. This type of study and information may save a great deal of lost time in the future.

It May Not Be a Do-It-Yourself Situation

Turning around a company that is in crisis mode usually requires outside help. We have seen this when we have been called in to help the turnaround effort. It is often the case that management has been too close to and too identified with the causes of the failure to see the forest for the trees. Furthermore, most managers have no experience with crisis management. There is a tendency to rely on legal advice-advice which is better at telling you what you can do, but not what you should do. Many lawyers are quite good at showing you how to exit a business with the least amount of damage, but they rarely can show you how to make your company successful once again. All too often, their advice will steer your company toward bankruptcy to set the stage for reorganization and restructure.

There are many things management can do before a company considers a Chapter 11 bankruptcy. This is not legal advice; it is management advice. Not only do you cede control to the lawyers, accounts, and consultants; but you may find that the costs involved further weaken the company and reduce the likelihood of recovery. It is commonly stated that a company has to have a lot of money to go bankrupt.

If achieving positive cash flow and simply paying the bills have turned into threatening problems, there are ways to restructure debt that do not require filing bankruptcy. In the process, both credit and credibility may be restored. When sales decline and receivables are slow or impossible to collect, the lack of capital makes it necessary to do some serious debt restructuring. A wrong decision at this point could easily mean the end of the company.

> **"Growth by itself does not guarantee profits."**

Keeping firmly in mind that bad cash flow is a symptom and not the cause of the problem, it is futile to search in a panic for a cash flow panacea. Moreover, it is an act of courage and wisdom for management to admit that it cannot do what needs to be done without help. Logically, the problem would not exist in the first place if management had the tools to fix the problem already in place. The only consideration should be: what is management willing to do to save jobs and to save the company.

The Voice of Experience

When I am called in as a consultant to repair a failing business, of course I ask management what the problem is as they see it. Usually I start hearing about dried up cash flow, not being able to pay the employees on time, having problems with creditors, and the like. My first job, then, is to get management to understand that what they are describing is not the problem, it is a symptom. Poor or non-existent cash flow is not what caused the business to founder. Something caused the cash flow to dry up, and that "something" is the problem. Often, clients want me to help them secure new financing. But, quick fixes don't last. Once management is clear on that, the real progress begins. The next step is to determine exactly what it was that caused the cash flow problem. There are a great number of things it might be. The problem might stem from ineffective sales and marketing. It might have come from extending too much credit to high risk customers. Maybe it was failure to establish a corporate culture of teamwork and mutual appreciation. It might have begun with unwise expansion into areas that were beyond the expertise of management. It might be the result of bad customer service. Determining the solution means understanding the problem.

Once the problem has been determined, it is time to make a plan and to take action. Emergency measures undertaken must consider the needs of all stakeholders in the business—creditors, employees, suppliers, customers, and shareholders. This should illustrate the futility of searching for the magic bullet. The problem is multi-faceted and must be approached in the same manner to the satisfaction of all concerned. Transparency is mandatory. Everyone involved will be more supportive if they can see some corrective action taking place. Quite often, employees know what's going on. They have a keen sense of the problems. And they often have some great suggestions for solutions.

Creditors, suppliers, employees, customers, and shareholders want and need to see a plan to correct the bad situation. That is not some kind of super business management 101. It is just human nature. If something has been wrong, people want to know what is going to be done about it. Just having a thought-out plan will go a long way toward reassuring stakeholders and buying additional time for management to effect the turnaround.

.Once the plan is a reality, it is now necessary to implement it with perseverance and hard work. The plan is only the starting point. It is useless if no corrective action is taken. Furthermore, the changes in the plan must be seen as permanent. If people see the changes as temporary, they will resist and even sabotage the changes while they wait for business to return to "normal". This is deadly to the success of the turnaround effort. The plan must not allow for a return to the old ways of doing business. Remembering that human nature is resistant to change, it will take a committed and determined management to drive the new plan forward. It's not an easy task. It is a collective effort to put into place a new and better way of doing things. It will require everyone's participation and support.

The new model can only be proven successful when the business begins to see happy customers, motivated employees, positive cash flow, and profitability. Obviously, such results cannot be expected overnight.   But, each small success will reassure suppliers, creditors, and employees. Success can snowball just as failure can.

Employee morale will be restored by the new teamwork effort where there is evidence that the company will rise again. When employees have a clear view of the effort being put in by management to saving their jobs and the company, their enthusiasm and participation will grow. They will be more willing to wait for pay raises and promotions if they see a company that has made a successful recovery.

Suppliers will be more accommodating and may even be willing to extend more credit when there is a clear indication that the company will recover and prosper once again.   Customer confidence will return when they have reason to believe the products they buy today will not be orphaned tomorrow. As cash flow improves and the dispursements of that new cash are handled wisely, the company can start making realistic projections about its return to profitability.

Then, and only then, the company is ready to move forward by adding capacity, new employees, and new physical plant. Scaling up a successful company is the best way to grow a company. Growth by itself does not guarantee profits.   But a profitable business model will create a positive return at any size.

Silver Linings Do Exist

Time and again I have worked with companies that recognize the need for both advice and change if they are going to survive. Those companies find a way to correct their mistakes and to bounce back stronger than ever. Turnarounds, and especially bankruptcies, are never fun and never to be taken lightly. But, they are learning experiences. In fact, they have to be in order for the company not to repeat the mistakes of the past. For companies and their managers who are willing to do the hard work of instituting change, the good news is that the future can be bright. There is light at the end of the tunnel, and it is not headlights.

But, too often some managers want the quick fix, the fad solution, without rooting out and correcting the problem. They and their companies muddle along never reaching their potential, and wonder why their luck was so bad. Too bad. The shareholders, the employees, and the customers deserve better.

Make no mistake about it, however. Making companies work is work. The same hard work that went into starting the business will be needed to fix the business and then to regrow the business. It calls for discipline and determination, both of which may have been lacking as the company slid downhill. It calls for devoted and loyal teamwork which means employees should expect reciprocal devotion and loyalty. But, it's worth it. As customers, it's not just about the product. As employees, it's not just about the paycheck. And, as good managers, it's not just about financial statements. It's about the pride you feel when you've served your customers well. And when you are the customer, it's the delight you feel from being taken care of.

Keys to this Chapter

Most managers are fired because of their inability or unwillingness to adapt to change.

You can't cut your way to prosperity. Downsizing is a temporary solution for a company in crisis.

There is a simple model for turning around a troubled company:

1. Handle the crisis. Get cash flow positive ASAP.

2. Find out what the real problem is.

3. Develop and implement a plan to correct the problems and create profit in the new, smaller company.

4. When the new model has proven to be profitable, then and only then, begin to expand the business to make more money.

Growth does not create profit

Growing an unprofitable dysfunctional company only results in a larger company that is more dysfunctional and usually more unprofitable.

Chapter Eleven

It's Cheaper to Keep 'Em

In many of the businesses I have worked with the fundamental problem is not the manager's lack of expertise or the staff's lack of motivation. The primary problem is the lack of a big picture mentality. The executives and/or owners have a short-term focus. As we wrote before, this focus is at most on the next quarter's results. Often, the focus can be measured in weeks, days, or even hours. This looks like managing by crisis where the leader is busy all day dealing with the small but urgent problems that every business faces. Ask most managers what they spend their time on, and they'll tell you it's "putting out fires".

This focus on the next fire leaves managers feeling helpless and lacking control over their companies' direction. It's common for these managers to lose sight of their purpose. There is even an aphorism that reminds us that when you are up to your eyeballs in alligators, it's difficult to remember that your objective was to drain the swamp. But, this is how it is in most companies. When you spend your days on these mini-emergencies, you forget purpose, you forget mission, and you forget your vision. This is how companies get into trouble.

The remedy for this is two-fold: first, executives need to learn how to let go, how to delegate, how to stop being firefighters. By definition, executives do no "work" in the physical sense. Executives organize, direct, coordinate, and communicate. But most of all, they lead. Every hour spent working is an hour not available for leading. Second, executives can lead only if they know where they are going. That requires direction. Direction comes from purpose, mission, and vision. It's not a matter of executives taking time from their jobs to work on the company's direction. Fulfilling the purpose, mission, and vision of the company is the executive's job. Executives and their managers need to revisit these every day to keep the organization on course.

In aviation, this problem is known as "flying the needle". Beginning pilots tend to overcorrect the airplane's altitude while trying to fly straight and level. Using the needle indicator on the altimeter, they pull back on the yoke whenever the altitude goes down and push forward on the yoke whenever the altitude goes up. The result is anything but straight and level flight. Instead, the airplane moves through the sky on a roller coaster path because the pilot was looking too closely at the situation. The answer in flying is to focus on the horizon. Concentrating on the big picture of where you want the airplane to go will help the pilot fly at a constant altitude. This same principle applies to "flying" a company.

When executives keep the horizon in mind, they stay aware of their companies' purpose, mission, and vision. Problems occur, setbacks happen, but the company quickly gets back on track. Even flaws in the business model can be recognized early and corrected when the leaders are focused on the end result. This long-term focus also prevents a lot of the secondary mistakes leaders make: the search for a quick fix, the susceptibility to fads, and the temptation to treat employees as just another disposable asset.

During a slowdown, one of the first panic buttons usually hit is the cost cutting button. Without logic or rationale, costs are cut anywhere possible. In many companies, payroll is the first "cost" to be cut. In a union shop, the rule of thumb is last-in-first-out (LIFO) which removes the newer, less experienced, and lowest paid employees. That leaves the employees with seniority and higher pay in place, so the cost structure is hardly affected at all.

The cost cutting and layoff combination has actually made little difference in either the cash flow or the profit margin.

In a non-union company the layoff process is reversed but still has unintended consequences. In these companies, the first to go are the more experienced, and more highly paid staff. This has the effect of staffing the company with less experienced employees who lack product knowledge, who have not been enculturated, who have not developed any company loyalty, and who have not developed strong customer relationships. Costs have been cut, but at considerable damage to the organization. The organization appears to the world to be disorganized and directionless. Many long-time, loyal customers no longer feel a connection to the company because they now are served by strangers. Many of these customers will leave to do business with companies that appear at least to be more stable.

> **"Downsizing and layoffs are always *the*
> *fault of management."***

In either of the above cases, the picture is not pleasant. The headlong rush to cut costs and layoff people cuts a swath through the business and leaves it in a more vulnerable position. Amazingly, many companies hire new employees even as they are laying off others. These companies suffer loss of intellectual capital and goodwill while their ex-employees suffer loss of jobs and incomes. But these costs are not offset by any monetary savings. It's amazing that these companies stay in business. But it all evens out. These same companies are usually takeover targets someday when another management team decides it can do a better job of running this company. They're probably right. Hiring through the front door while firing through the back door amounts to managerial incompetence. It has no significant effect on savings but does damage to the ex-employees and demoralizes remaining staff.

Consider the Benefits

There are many benefits to retaining and retraining existing employees as opposed to using layoffs to cut costs:

- Working to retain employees reassures employees of the company's loyalty to them. Management that does not consider the morale of the workers is mismanagement. When employees see that management is making every effort to provide job security to the staff, morale remains high. There is a greater willingness for employees to pitch in and do their part to save the company and their jobs. Employee enthusiasm and loyalty are wonderful during good times. They are mandatory during down times.

- Retraining employees is cheaper than outplacement, recruiting, and training new employees. It's not just smarter; it's cheaper. Training new employees means starting from the ground up, indoctrinating them into the company culture, and training through the mistakes that are made due to inexperience. Retraining existing employees simply means adding new skills to existing and well practiced skills.

- Additionally, the ability of existing employees to be trained is known. They have all gone through the introductory company training and have settled in as permanent employees. Not everyone who is hired will last even 90 days. No matter how carefully you screen prospective employees, they are still unproven as workers and contributors. They are unknown quantities. Some of them may not be trainable at all. Every time a new hire fails to grasp the company training and cannot pass the initial probationary period, it means that the whole process from recruitment to training must start all over again.

- The existing workers in a business are generally older and more mature. These are people who are more reliable. They have less absenteeism and are normally the group most likely to be loyal to the product, the company, and the customers.

- Not the least of the advantages of retaining existing employees is their knowledge of the customers, the products, and the corporate culture. Those employees who deal directly with the customer are the real face of the company. Most customers would not know the CEO if they tripped over him on the sidewalk. But they remember the employee who helped them make the right purchase from a large line of products, who took time to explain the proper use of the product, who helped them get large items out the door and into their cars, or who arranged for speedy delivery of items that could not be carried out. Such customer focus can be developed. Hiring it off the street is rare.

Downsizing and Layoffs are *Always* the Fault of Management

Managers who suffer from over inflated egos are bound to make the mistakes that require downsizing and layoffs. Bloated egos lead to bloated companies. Then these managers are further rewarded when they try to correct their own mistakes by laying off workers. Good leaders and responsible managers see themselves as servants or stewards of their companies. To these leaders every business is a people business. And good leaders don't get rid of their people any more than they would get rid of their customers. Daniel McCafferty, General Manager of the luxury Dusit Thani Hotel in Bangkok, Thailand is a classic example of a manager who values his team as much as his customers He occupies a small office with furniture that is nice but modest. He is seldom in the office, however. Instead, he spends his days walking around the hotel observing the service, talking to managers, and conferring with his department heads. He knows each of his 1,000 employees by name. He mixes with the guests and invites their comments about the facilities and service. *Layoff* is not in his vocabulary.

Here, then, are the characteristics of a good manager:

- Good managers practice appropriate hiring. This involves both quality and quantity. A good manager will authorize hiring only when the additional capacity is truly needed. There is no empire building on his or her watch where hiring is done simply to satisfy the ego of a department head. In boom times the good manager will not approve new hiring when the forecast does not indicate sustainability of the boom. Hiring may be the function of the HR department, but it is always the *responsibility* of management.

▪ Good managers understand the constant need for training. Workers need training to be more productive. From time to time, they need refresher training. Job skills training, customer service training, ethics training, emergency response training, and any area of the business that improves the ability of the company to attract and retain customers is essential.

▪ The good manager is never the last one to know about problems within the organization. The job of the manager is to manage and to lead. He or she cannot do that without being attuned to everything that goes on within the company. That means two-way communication from top to bottom, from executive suite to factory floor. It cannot be done by memo or intranet. It is sleeves-rolled-up involvement that alerts the manager to problems or potential problems.

▪ Another area that falls under the management umbrella is the retraining and refocusing to meet the challenges of change in the marketplace. This involves having a finger on the pulse of the expanding current markets and methods for capturing new markets. This simply means that the effective manager will not only know what is going on inside the company but will also be aware of what is happening in the outside world.

Layoffs and downsizing are not a long-term solution to poor management. They are evidence that management failed to take the long view and is now having to respond to short-term exigencies. Unfortunately, the pain of that failure is most often felt by the employees. It is unconscionable that executives get pay raises and bonuses while laying off their employees. But they do. Executives are then rewarded for trying to correct their own mismanagement. They are praised for failure to redeploy their most valuable and most expensive company assets—their employees. It's not difficult to understand why many employees have become jaded and skeptical of management.

As this book was written, the highly publicized decision by Circuit City to fire approximately 4,000 of it most highly paid sales people hit the media. The public outcry was loud and sustained for the callous treatment of the employees and the customers who had come to rely on the employees' expertise and personal service. The reason given for the firings was to cut payroll costs. However, in some cases the wage differential between the experienced employees and the new hires was reported to be as little as $1-2 per hour. Furthermore, departing employees were granted four to eight weeks severance pay. While the severance pay is thoughtful, it negates much of the near-term cost savings. Thousands of people lost their jobs for a corporate benefit that may or may not occur in the future.

Predictably, the new employees hired to replace those experienced and knowledgeable employees who were shown the door will expect pay raises as their tenure grows and they become more knowledgeable about company products. What will happen to them? Will they receive raises for good and faithful service? Will their fate be the same as their predecessors? Will they also be fired as soon as they earn their way to higher pay grades? The alternative is to recruit a cohort of workers who have no hope of getting raises. Either way-get raises and get fired or work forever at the same pay-Circuit City can expect recruiting to be more difficult, turnover to be higher, and motivation to be non-existent. We'd be interested to learn who besides the CEO got a bonus for this decision.

We have long argued that layoffs rarely save a company money in the long run. We are not talking about layoffs of temporary and seasonal workers who understand the limits of their tenure. Rather, we are talking about layoffs or reductions in force among workers who thought they were permanent employees-people who wanted careers and not just jobs.

Elicit Help from the Team

CEOs often complain that if they tell employees what is really going on in the company, the employees will bolt. They will quit and leave the company worse off. Our experience has been the opposite. Employees bail on a company when management has created an environment of limited communication, has an us versus them mentality, and has fostered an atmosphere of mutual distrust. In companies that treat their employees as team members and shoot straight with them, the employees will not only stay, they will work even harder to help the company fix the problems. It is a huge mistake for managers to underestimate their people when the chips are down.

> *"The best way to keep payroll costs down is to improve the retention of your workforce."*

When Colleen Barrett, President of Southwest Airlines, faced the difficulties after 9/11, she wasted no time meeting with the employees. She worked overtime to assure them that Southwest would do everything possible before considering layoffs. Everyone went happily back to work and Southwest Airlines weathered the storm. There is no advantage in keeping people in the dark. If you trust your people in adversity, they will respond and work with you. It is one of the many benefits of true teamwork.

The difficult thing about discussing bad business conditions with employees is that management often has to admit the fact that lax management created the problem in the first place. But regardless of whether management wants to accept responsibility, employees usually know the score. Passing the buck or dancing around the issues serves only to earn the scorn and disrespect of your team. Sharing with them honestly what they probably already know creates stronger bonds and more motivated employees. They understand that you get it. And since you are the leader, positive change will not happen until you do get it. These situations are no time for posturing or ego protection.

Sharing the Sacrifices

When faced with the possibility of cutbacks and layoffs, employees respond positively to management that is also willing to forego raises, bonuses, and perks. It still astonishes me that executives are paid bonuses for running a company into the ground. A modicum of common sense should tell CEOs and boards of directors that granting managers raises and bonuses while asking for employee wage concessions is not a formula for loyalty and cooperation. It is a slap in the face to your employees. It is also poor leadership, poor management, and poor public relations. Beyond the moral issue, SEC disclosure rules make it possible now for employees and the public to find out this previously obscure information. Dumb on a number of counts.

People Create Profitability

Studies have shown repeatedly that companies that pay attention to people issues within the organization have the highest rate of employee commitment to the company. Furthermore, those same studies show that those companies have outperformed other companies during difficult times. Those companies enjoy a low turnover rate. Make no mistake, turnover is expensive.

More emphasis on the people within the company results in higher profit margins as well. One study has estimated an average return 66 percent higher. One of our most admired companies, Southwest Airlines, is a good example of this.

The reason behind the success of a people-oriented business is simple. Business is people. Only people do actual work. Only people sell your products. And only people buy the products.

These simple-minded statements are more profound than many executives think. In today's age of high-tech, we get carried away by the latest ecommerce technology, the most advanced robots, the coolest software and databases. But none of these buy or sell stuff. Only people initiate transactions. Everything else is just a tool to facilitate those transactions. Thus, the wise manager will put people first: the employers and the customers. And included in the philosophy is a commitment by management to keep its eye on the long-term ball; a commitment to run the company with purpose, mission, and vision so that the day never arrives when the boss has to tell his employees, "I screwed up: you're fired".

In the current business environment of acquisitions, divestitures, downsizings, and reductions in force, the media have reported that 60% of American workers do not trust the management of the companies they work for. That's a sad commentary on the mood of the American workforce. And, it's an indictment of those managers who pay lip service to the notion of teamwork and loyalty.

Communication Instead of Layoffs

Here is the way to fix a struggling business: talk to your employees. Tell them the truth. Ask for their support, and their ideas. They know more about the problem than you think they do. American Airlines pilots did not simply blindly accept pay cuts. There was communication and understanding between management and the pilots association. The employees of Southwest Airlines did not automatically put on happy faces and turn off their brains after the attacks on 9/11. They listened to management; they trusted, and they performed.

Instead of considering what the business can do *to* employees during difficult times, management needs to consider what can be done *for* the employees. How might matters have turned out differently at Circuit City if this principle had been applied? People like to be given choices and to be made to feel that they have something to contribute to the company. Suppose the executives had all taken pay cuts to help save the company. Of course, they would still have had their jobs. But the point is this: if team has any meaning in a modern corporation, it has to mean that what affects one affects all. All share the ups and the downs, the pay cuts and the pay raises. Anything less reinforces the notion that there are workers, and then there are the privileged few. And when one group thrives while the other group suffers, you have a recipe for low morale and high turnover. It's bad business, and it's not right.

Symbolism is a non-verbal but yet powerful type of communication. It's true that management pay cuts will not significantly improve cash flow in most cases. But, that's not the point. What is important is the demonstration of senior management to sacrifice along with the rank and file. If top management is willing to bear the same burdens they require of staff in order to stall layoffs, most employees will be more willing to cooperate. Those who choose to walk out are no big loss since they obviously have little or no loyalty to the company in the first place. It follows that a management willing to share the hard times should also be willing to share the profits and benefits. The example of Bill Greehey at Valero is a case in point. If the CEO gets a bonus, every employee of the company gets a bonus. Yes, it may mean the CEOs bonus is smaller that way, but it will pay great dividends in the long haul.

Looking for the Long Range Picture

Companies don't fail without reasons. It's not bad luck. It's not even a bad workforce. After all, who hired the workers? Management needs to look in the mirror for its problems. Many failing companies have deep-seated, systemic problems. Short-term thinking and short-term solutions continue the mismanagement that caused the distress in the first place. Keeping employees and looking for other ways to cut costs, increase sales, and return to profitability is the correct approach. It is not a quick fix, but it's a good fix. It may even be painful for a while. It requires a different way of thinking and different ways of doing things. It requires overcoming resistance to change. Correcting a poor business model that led to a crisis situation is more effort and more difficult than following sound business principles in the first place. But, you do what it takes, and hope you've learned from the experience.

> ## *"You don't lose employees; you drive them away."*

It's Cheaper to Keep 'em

The cost of recruiting, hiring, and training new employees is enormous. It can cost the company as much as a year's pay to replace a lost worker. The best way to keep payroll costs down is to improve the retention of your workforce. But just like customer retention, more money is spent on acquiring new employees than on retaining existing employees. We're not talking about raises and bonuses here. We're talking about recognition. Recognition can include monetary rewards, but usually does not. Recognition can be as inexpensive as a heartfelt "Thank you". In fact, there seems to be an inverse relationship between pay and recognition. The less the recognition and appreciation, the more money employees want. Cash becomes a form of appreciation, but it is poor one. People work for more than money. They do not constantly seek out the highest paying employers. Survey after survey shows that employees want reasonable pay. They're not after every last dollar they can get. Once they feel they are earning a fair salary, employees want meaningful work, respect from their teams, and recognition for their contributions. It is a colossal management mistake to think that money is a motivator and that people work primarily for money. In fact, just paying more money is the easy way out. It is far more difficult to find and train managers who have the empathy and people skills that employees value. It's worth it to find those managers and hire them. It's also worth it to develop this in your team.

Employee retention has always been important to a company's success. Now it is critical. There is increased competition for good employees-employees who are team players, self-motivated, and driven by a personal sense of excellence. That competition makes it increasingly difficult to recruit them. So it just makes good business sense to know how to retain them once you've hired them. In fact, employee retention is becoming a strategic advantage in all industries. Companies are increasingly aware that keeping good people will enhance productivity and keep the true cost of labor to a minimum, even while paying above average salaries. If you spend less money on employee turnover, you have more money to spend on your existing team. And you will still save money.

What Makes Employees Stay?

In the last twenty years, job changing-what some used to call job hopping-has become commonplace. There is no longer a stigma to changing jobs every few years. In some industries such as high tech, it is expected. Some of this job changing is caused by younger workers wanting to climb the career ladder as quickly as possible. But much of the job changing is involuntary. Most people do not like to search for jobs. They hate writing resumes and attending job interviews. That means that there is a built-in "stickiness" to your employees. In most cases, when an employee quits your company, it's because something or someone drove him away. Sounds a lot like our customer discussion, doesn't it? You don't lose customers; you drive them away. Likewise, you don't lose employees; you drive them away as well. Few new hires keep their resumes up to date and at the ready. They start to explore the job market only when something threatens their job security or when they see turmoil and favoritism at work.

Some companies also push people out the door when their managers try to implement QC or efficiency programs. Quality and productivity are extremely important, of course. The problem arises when managers impose an abrupt change or bureaucracy with its attendant forms and checklists. Previously happy employees have told me that they once enjoyed their jobs. They would work extra hours and go the extra mile to complete a project or help the company through a rough time. But employee attitudes sour quickly when management latches on to the latest fad by requiring detailed time sheets or lists of daily activities. There is a fine line between tracking employee productivity and treating your work staff like slackers. Employees who feel like they are suspects in their own companies begin thinking the previously unthinkable. They begin to imagine working somewhere else. Most employees make the decision to leave long before they have given notice. That period between decision and final day can be a period of lower productivity and disruption caused by the lack of loyalty from the soon-to-be ex-employee. Taking care of your employees doesn't just reduce the costs of turnover, it is good prevention practice.

Employees maintain company loyalty when they are treated with respect and made to feel that they are important to the success of the company. Management actions that treat employees as factors of production just don't work. Recruiting, training, and keeping good people is a lot of work. But the differences between a worker and a motivated team member make it all worthwhile.

Employees also want to feel secure in the knowledge that their managers are looking out for their interests. They are more loyal when they know there is someone in their corner ready to go to bat for them when needed. One way of giving employees a better feeling of security is periodic, relevant feedback and training. Some people will become better trained and use that training to move to another company. Most will not. The money spent on employee training and education is not wasted. The ROI on employee education is high. And, when you consider that it is so hard to find qualified and motivated people, it makes good business sense and good financial sense to develop the people you already have. Your current employees have already passed your HR filters. They have become a part of the corporate culture. And, they have shown some loyalty by staying with you. You don't need to look far and wide for wonderful team members. You can grow them yourself with the people you have.

Finally, employee retention goes up when employees are kept in the loop of communication. Managers who are accessible to the employees, listen intently to the employees, and speak directly and honestly create an atmosphere of open communication that is lacking in so many organizations, but is prized by employees. Workers understand that they may not get everything they want, but they appreciate being heard. And this open communication doesn't cost the company a dime. Employee retention doesn't have to cost a lot of money. In the best run companies, it doesn't.

Don't Have to Sell the Farm

During the writing of this book, a heretofore unimaginable event occurred in the business world. General Motors, for decades the world's largest and dominant automaker, was overtaken by Toyota. Incredibly, the news of GM's number two status was greeted with little fanfare and even less commentary. Normally, such a change would evoke howls of anguish throughout the country-a what-is-the-world-coming-to questioning of America's industrial downfall. Instead, the change in auto leadership was almost a footnote in the business press. Sadly, the reason for the indifference is that the change has been anticipated for a long time. This was no sudden cataclysm. No unexpected upheaval; no act of nature. Instead, this change marked the long, slow decline of a company that had lost its way. A company that lost touch with its customers. The list of management errors over the past three decades is a long one. One particular blunder is relevant here.

As the Japanese car and truck manufactures began their push to penetrate the American market, a defensive backlash developed that cried, "Buy American". People bought American cars solely on the idea that American cars and trucks were better because they were made in America. No matter that many American makes and models were more expensive and were lower quality vehicles. Patriotism ruled. The cry back then was "if they (the Japanese) were building their cars in America, they could not sell them as cheap as they do now." In an attempt to level the auto playing field, import duties were placed on Japanese cars to make them as overpriced as the American cars. But still, Americans bought Japanese cars in increasing numbers. The import duties did accomplish one thing: they spurred the Japanese auto makers to build assembly plants here in the U.S. By building their vehicles in this country, they could continue to sell their products at the same price as before. But now they could, in effect, pocket the import duties themselves. But, something else happened that was to have the biggest impact on Japanese auto makers' success and GM's (and Ford's and Chrysler's) decline. Americans realized that Hondas and Toyotas were now "Made in America". Oops. There went the last obstacle to buying so-called foreign cars.

> ***"Downsizing the workforce is an admission that your business model doesn't work."***

Now here is where it gets into the "what were they thinking?" category. While Toyota was building sparkling new factories in places where the labor union was not strong, Detroit's auto management was capitulating to the unions and agreeing to ruinous labor contracts. Toyota, in the meantime, could use its labor cost advantage to continually improve their product's quality. After all, when comparable models sell for the same price, you can only spend the same amount to build your car as can your competitor. And when you pay $70 an hour for labor while your competitor pays "only" $35 an hour, something has to give. That something, for American car makers, was quality. Here is an example of cheaper-to-keep-em gone awry. Keeping the workforce was done at the expense of quality. And, it was at the expense of giving customers what they wanted: more convenience, better styling, and higher quality. This was a company that was run for the benefit of management and labor. Everyone forgot the customer. Except the Japanese. Another reminder to take care of your employees, but the reason you are in business is to serve the customers.

Look at the Reverse Side

Ostensibly, the reason for cut backs in the workforce is to save money by cutting costs. It seldom if ever accomplishes that end. Cutting staff is a bandage, not a cure. Downsizing the workforce is an admission that your business model doesn't work. Unless something changes in the way the company does business, future hirings will lead only to future layoffs. Cutting employees is not the answer to the real problem.

When a company has to downsize, it is fighting a battle for survival much like when an army goes to war. If you were to go into battle, who would you rather have with you: new recruits or battle hardened veterans. Keeping the best, most experienced employees and enlisting their cooperation in addressing the causes of the downturn is the sensible solution. Retaining good employees and putting a freeze on new hiring while attacking the actual problem does not generate headlines. In these cases, CEOs are not considered heroes. They do not get bonuses for making the "tough decisions". They just quietly marshal their troops and attack the real problems. It isn't glamorous, but it is heroic. And, it is the best way to make companies work.

Keys to this Chapter

🔑 Keep your eyes on the real prize: that prize is your purpose, your mission, and your vision.

🔑 Ask yourself and your management team every day, "What are we trying to accomplish?"

🔑 Employees are not expendable. It is expensive to get rid of them and even more costly to replace them. Most companies can't afford to layoff employees if they want to stay in business.

🔑 Layoffs cut costs less than you think. And, you lose the intellectual capital and loyalty of the employees. It's cheaper to keep them.

🔑 Short term solutions only fix short term problems. Getting a company back on track may involve making over the company. This isn't reengineering. This is survival. Vow to get it right this time. Many times an outside perspective can help.

Chapter Twelve

The Secret of Greatness: Legendary Customer Service

Everything we've covered in this book is important to the success of a company. But the primary determinant of long-term success is the ability to deliver excellent customer service. When we talk about making companies work we mean making companies fulfill their purpose which is to satisfy the needs and wants of customers. Without customers, there is no business. Yet all too often, customers have been largely overlooked or reduced to impersonal numbers. Customer turnover cannot completely be avoided, but the main reason for that turnover is that companies chase customers away by indifferent or even hostile customer service.

The Real Purpose of Business

The real purpose of business is to satisfy the wants and needs of customers. Despite what business schools teach, the purpose of business is NOT to provide a profit to the owners/shareholders. Profit is the result and the reward for being of service to customers. If a company were in business primarily or solely to make a profit, it would sell the lowest quality products that it could get away with. It would ignore customer service as long as product returns cost less than its profit. Come to think of it, that describes a lot of companies today. Most of them don't last very long because taking advantage of customers is not a viable long-term business model. Let's say it another way: the key to long-term business success is to serve customers. As we've written before, the true purpose of any company is to satisfy the wants and needs of customers and thereby earn a profit. And being a great company requires delivering great customer service. Profit is a necessary part of this definition for good reasons:

- Without profit, the business cannot continue to operate
- Profit enables a business to attract further capital
- Profit provides funds for expansion and reinvestment.

The point is that profit is the result of finding out what people want and then getting it to them. Ideally, it means providing excellent customer service that generates good will and repeat business. When profit becomes the focal point of a business it usually means the cheapest and poorest quality products are offered at the highest possible prices. The focus is on the interests of the company or its salespeople, and not on the best interests of the customers. Often, this misdirected model results in high pressure sales tactics and subsequent buyer remorse. Neither of these will create satisfied customers or repeat business. Therefore, it is not a long-term business model.

Here is an example most people can relate to. The story involves an elderly relative. A salesman comes to the home of the relative to explain the benefits of some new vacuum cleaner or cookware. Typically, the old vacuum cleaner or cookware is just fine, but no matter. There are commissions to be earned, sales contests to be won, and victories to be achieved by the salesman. The relative, on the other hand, is too timid or too polite to turn the salesman away. So the salesman talks. And talks and talks. He won't give up. He won't leave. Finally, the relative is worn down and buys the product just to end the high sales pressure. A day or two later, when the relative tries to cancel the order or return the product, the company ignores the request or stalls. The relative is stuck with a product she didn't need at a price five times retail. Maybe it's happened to you.

The story is an example of a company that has put profit as its sole purpose. Sales are recorded and profits are made, but the aftermath is buyer remorse and bad feelings toward the company. It's difficult to see this as a sustainable business model. This is customer disservice.

The Employees as Number One

I have heard at least one CEO proudly make the statement that in his company, employees are number 1 and customers are number 2. Really? If that were true, the company business hours would all be scheduled around the needs of the employees rather than those of the customers. Perhaps 9 am-5 pm Mondays through Fridays with no nights, weekends, or holidays. Prices, policies, and locations would all be set arbitrarily to fit some manager's notion of fair prices and fair profit. Customer service? Take a number, and get in line. We'll get to you when we get to you. The needs of customers would be unimportant. Sounds ridiculous, doesn't it? Yet we already have an example of that model. It's called government. Think Post Office or the DMV offices. Nobody thinks of these agencies as customer oriented. We use them because we have no choice. Government can get away with such disregard for customer service because it is an enduring monopoly. This is what you get when the employees come first.

> *"The real purpose of business is to satisfy the wants and needs of customers."*

There is no denying that good employees are vital to the success of any business. Much of our emphasis has been on taking care of your employees and treating them as the important assets they are. However, the employees can NOT be number 1 on the priority list. Customers enter a business establishment to spend their money on something that will satisfy their needs. They are not coming in to satisfy the needs of the employees of the company. They come to transact business—not to donate to a charity.

Customer Focus: The Top Priority

Not everyone, obviously, agrees that customers are the number 1 concern of any business. That explains why so many businesses disappear after just a few years. These companies have been focused on something other than the customer:

- **Product focus** is often where the attention lies. Software and high tech companies are notorious for this, but many other companies are product driven. Customers don't buy products. It's a cliché-but a true one-that customers buy solutions. We take that one step further: customers buy experiences. They want the experience of making their lives easier, more profitable, or more efficient. If they are consumers, they also want the experience to be entertaining. The product may well be excellent. But the product is only a device that facilitates the experience. If your company is product driven, you are vulnerable to a competitor's me-too product, or even to a superior product. But if your focus is on the customer's total experience, your product becomes only one part of customer satisfaction.

  Consumers don't want DVD players, for example. They really don't care to buy a metal box filled with electronic gizmos. They want to enjoy movies. Customers don't go to most restaurants for the food. They go for the socializing, the service of the wait staff, the convenience of not cooking and leaving the dishes behind. Case in point: how many people go to restaurants alone? And don't people like to eat where there are a lot of other people? If it were the food, an empty restaurant would be preferable. No crowds, no noise, no busy waiters. Cosmetics, cars, jewelry-all are sold for something other than their utility. Customers buy the dream, the image, the respect and envy of their friends. Next time you watch television, don't flip through the commercials. Pay attention to what the advertisers are really selling. They're selling health, fun, good experiences, and good memories.

- **Employee focus** relegates the customer to second class citizenship. Customers find that they cannot get shopping assistance or have to wait in a long checkout line because the employees are busy doing something else. This same principle applies as well to internet shopping sites that are complicated to navigate and difficult to shop. It is the internet equivalent of getting no personal help in the store and having to wait in a long line at the register. But the tech staff sure thinks the site is smokin'.

- **Executive focus** satisfies the needs of management with bonuses and stock options that may give executives warm, fuzzy feelings but leave customers and employees cold. The business becomes something of a game, the object of which is to see how much executives can get out of it for themselves. As we discussed in Chapter One, this is Greedership, not Leadership. Unfortunately, we're all reading more and more reports of Greedership in the business press. Greedership is becoming so outrageous the popular media are now catching on and making it a hot topic.

- **Stock price focus** is common but misguided. Shareholders are complicit because they think they benefit from stock price focus. But most shareholders are long-term buy-and-hold investors. Since stock price focus is a short-term strategy, these long-term investors usually get shortchanged. There are some accounting tricks, sales tricks, even reporting tricks CEOs can use to boost stock prices in the short run. But long-term success and long-term sustainable profit is based on delivering excellent customer service and value.

The simple fact is that most companies today focus on just about anything except the customer. They may say that they are customer oriented, but their actions speak louder than their words.

In most companies, the employees who actually deal with the customers are usually the youngest and least experienced. They have the least knowledge about the products, they are the least mature, and they are the least career-minded employees. They are not customer-centric. But these are the people companies rely on to care for their precious customers.

> *"The simple fact is that most companies today focus on just about anything except the customer."*

It is Not Just Handling Complaints

It is amazing how so many companies equate customer service with handling complaints. Not only that, the approach they take is to dispatch the complainers as quickly as possible. Such an attitude is wrong on two counts. First, legitimate complaints provide an opportunity to learn something that may improve the product, service, or both. Second, rushing a complainant out the door is chasing away a customer that will probably never return and will undoubtedly tell many people about the bad service at the company.

Customers who complain are doing your company a favor! They are providing you with valuable feedback that marketing departments pay millions of dollars for. When customers complain, you get this information for free. It is myopic to view customer service as only the resolution of complaints. And when your customer service staff share that view, it's easy to see why most employees dread working in customer service. When customers are unhappy yet don't tell you, when your employees make complainers feel unwelcome, you have a real problem. You may think the lack of complaints is a good sign, but it usually means that customers are leaving without telling you why. Worse, since you didn't know, you have no opportunity to fix the problem.

A key part of our customer service consulting is to train the employees to welcome customer complaints. You never want to disappoint customers or make them unhappy, of course. But you do want to know where your problems are. And, there's something else. When a customer complains, your company has a chance to show what it's made of: to demonstrate its integrity, its helpfulness, and its passion for taking care of its customers. Some of your best customers, your most loyal customers and your best missionaries, will come from dissatisfied customers made happy.

This is so important that it bears repeating: discouraging complaints or getting rid of complainers as quickly as possible is another short-sighted solution. It does not identify what went wrong in the customer relationship. But identifying the problem, correcting the problem, and satisfying the customer are how legendary brands are built. They are how companies become famous for their customer focus, and how they develop a competitive advantage in their industries.

Customer service, therefore, can be defined as people-to-people contact that requires excellent interpersonal skills. Members of our society as a whole have gotten worse at simply getting along with each other. Instead of meeting in person to accommodate each other, we sit in our homes or offices and email, instant message, and blog each other. Instead of socializing the way we used to, we sit at home and watch cable television. Alone in a house full of people. Several decades ago there was only one TV per household. Today, the average household has more TV's than inhabitants. Multiple TV's allow each family member to go to a separate room and watch TV alone. Browsing the internet, a solitary experience, now occupies a large portion of personal time. As a nation, we are spending less and less time on face-to-face interaction. Businesses have resorted to online chat that gives the illusion of personal contact but is really just a form of text messaging. Even that limited customer contact is complicated. First, the customer is expected to read the service bulletins or FAQs (Frequently Asked Questions) to see if the problem can be solved—alone. Then finding the link to initiate an online chat is often so obscure, the customer just gives up. What we are seeing here is not customer service; it is a technological wall to avoid customer contact.

Cut, Cut, Cut—A Huge Mistake

Most companies view customer service as a cost center to the company. To curry the favor of Wall Street when the focus is on stock prices, those companies look for ways to cut costs. One of the first cuts, often, is the customer service center. Many times the cost-cutting leads to outsourcing to a company that knows neither the language nor the culture. The message to customers is clear: we don't care about you. We certainly don't care enough to set up call centers that will actually solve your problems and take care of you. Clearly those companies do not recognize that excellent customer service contributes greatly to the top line as well as the bottom line profit of the business. They fail to recognize that customer service is an integral part of the income production chain. Customer service provides valuable input which is a necessary part of continued sales and the success of the organization. A company that seriously wants to grow sales and profits will not only avoid cutting customer service, but will invest *more* dollars into improved service until the company is best in its industry.

Examples of Abysmal Customer Service

Understanding what good customer service is may best be explained by what it is not. Look over this list by considering the times such events have happened to you and how you felt about them at the time:

1. **You visit a car repair shop** and drop off your automobile early in the morning for something that should take 2 hours to do. At 5:00 p.m., when you are ready to leave from work, the repair shop tells you the car will not be ready until tomorrow. They have had all day to give you a call and let you know there would be a delay, but they did not. Now you have no ride home and have to scramble to find a ride.

2. **The home repair company** schedules a call for Tuesday. You take off from work and stay at home all day, but the repairmen never show up. When you call, they tell you they were busy and did not get around to your house. There is not even an apology for wasting your valuable time.

3. **The cable TV company** has a 5-level phone menu. You are a prospective new customer waiting to subscribe with new business that will be worth over $1,000.00 a year for them. We have actually noted cable TV companies that put their sales line on the third level down. You have to drill down 3 levels just to place your order and give them your money. In one of our tests, it took 16 minutes to reach a human being who could take our order and our money. Of course, while you are waiting to spend your money with the company, you hear a recording that assures you how important your call is to them.

4. **Call many doctor's offices** today and you are likely to get an answer that goes automatically to a voicemail box. You are informed that if it is an emergency call 911. (That great advice could end up costing you thousands of dollars.) You do get to leave a message which may or may not be returned. In a survey of physicians' office we were able to talk to a person without talking to voice mail only 58%of the time. 40% of voicemail messages went unreturned within 24 hours.

5. **Any company that plays** the recorded message that says, "Your call is important to us. Please stay on the line. A customer service representative will be with you shortly." While you wait-we call it growing old on hold-the message thoughtfully keeps playing over and over while you sit drumming your fingers. The fact that the message has been "looped" to repeat endlessly indicates that the company knew your call would take a long time to be answered.

6. **A customer service representative** you finally reach cannot solve your problem. In fact, probably he or she

cannot solve *any* problem. This is known as a level one employee, a screener. If the call is not dropped, you are transferred to someone you are told can help you. Many times during the transfer, the line mysteriously gets disconnected. Telephone systems have been with us for 131 years, and yet a technology company can't transfer calls reliably. Or maybe your call just wasn't very important to them.

7. **The online salesperson** informs you that you cannot get the price posted on the website. You ask why not and are informed that the "price is out of date." Why has it not been changed? It begins to feel like the old bait and switch routine.

8. **You fill out a sales inquiry form** because you are actually interested in the product. No one ever contacts you. Research show that more than 50% of all sales leads are never followed up. It is a colossal waste of money to put that much into generating leads that are never utilized. It is an insult to the prospective customer who used his or her time to fill it out and then never heard back from the company. That missed sale is not waiting for you to call. That prospect has already bought from your competitor. He is probably lost to you forever.

9. **The server in a sandwich shop,** who has been talking loudly with other employees, or worse yet, on the phone, tells you they are "out of" something you ordered. You suspect there is plenty in the cooler, but it was easier to tell you they don't have the item than it was to look in inventory.

Notice that none of these examples involved actual product. The products may have been excellent. They may have been best-in-class. But you can't get through the poor service to get to the product. It's just too much trouble for you. So you leave. The company can spend all the money in the bank on product development, but it will be money wasted if their customer service is poor. Product driven companies do not get it.

> ## *"Customers who complain are doing your company a favor!"*

Why All the Emphasis on Excellent Customer Service?

Excellent Customer Service (ECS) is the bottom line secret to successful business. Whatever your personal feelings may be about Wal-Mart, it is undeniable that the company was founded on the principle of ECS. Sam Walton knew his market, the millions of middle-to-low income families who wanted and needed quality products at affordable prices. From the time customers were greeted at the door right up through checkout, they got a feeling of importance. Whatever Wal-Mart is today, it grew into its remarkable size from careful attention to the customers.

There are many reasons to make ECS the focal point of a business:

1. **Since most companies** are so poor at customer service, if you make it the main thrust of your company and do it well— not necessarily excellent, just well—your company will stand out from the crowd.

2. **ECS is a competitive edge** in today's business world where so few companies pay attention to the customer. You might also look at it as a strategic advantage. ECS is the best way to grow your company and to realize your corporate vision. ECS is a differentiator in the marketplace. Customers recognize their importance and compare the way you handle customer service favorably against those companies that do not.

3. **ECS helps define your brand.** There is no amount of advertising that can equal the effect excellent customer service has on defining a brand. The excellent service marks your brand as desirable and of high quality. A reputation for ECS creates a mental image of your brand

that strongly appeals to customers. When people buy, they always want to know how the business will stand behind their products. When the customer is treated as number 1 in the company priorities, they feel confident in buying the products.

4. **ECS is one of the best and cheapest** ways to enhance your company's reputation not only among current customers but also with prospective customers. The entire marketplace takes notice of the company that has an excellent people-to-people reputation.

5. **ECS is an input** and not an expense. The more spent on ECS, the greater the sales. Companies that emphasize ECS not only have more sales, but their profit margins are greater. By running the company well (see Chapters 8 and 10) and focusing on the customer, a business avoids the quick fix and the fad frenzy. Excellent customer service is the best path to long-term business success. An ECS company stands behind its products and services and does whatever it takes to satisfy the customer from initial contact to long after a sale is made. The rewards of that kind of service may not appear directly on an income statement, but they positively influence sales and profits.

6. **Being known for ECS** makes it much easier to sell to new customers. There is a lower perceived risk to buying a product when new customers are preconditioned to the company's customer-friendly philosophy. Success creates more success. Being successful at ECS paves the way for more sales to existing customers as well as new ones.

7. **Employees of a company** known for ECS have higher morale. Nobody wants to work for a company that has a poor reputation. No one enjoys having to hang his or her head when asked where they work. On the other side of that coin, however, are the proud employees who work for a company that has a stellar reputation for good products and excellent service. The employees observe that the customers are being treated in exactly the same way they

themselves would like to be treated when they are the customers.

8. **There is a multiplier effect** on overall quality of the business as the result of ECS. When service is top notch, it forces engineers, salespeople, and production workers to keep improving the product and the processes for making the product. That is exactly the kind of results any business would like to achieve. Excellence is not a department, a slogan, or a management fad. Truly excellent companies strive for excellence in every area. But first among these, should be service to the customers.

Just as excellence builds upon itself, so does mediocrity. Consider what happens when the company provides mediocre customer service. The result will be a great number of unhappy customers who never return. With no company reputation for customer service to uphold, there is little incentive to improve the products. It's easier to be excellent in all areas or mediocre in all areas. Excellence and mediocrity cannot long coexist.

Getting rid of customers, even difficult ones, is a costly practice. Just as it is cheaper to keep good employees (see Chapter 11), it is far, far cheaper to keep your old customers than it is to go out and try to replace them with new ones. The higher the number of customers lost the higher the number of new customers needed to maintain and then grow the business. That invariably means higher advertising costs and price cuts to attract the new customers.

Count the Costs

Companies spend a significant percentage of their revenues seeking new customers. To keep new customers coming in, expensive advertising is bought. Companies also try to attract new customers by running sales promotions, offering discounts, and spending large sums on public relations. But only a small percentage of prospects turn into paying customers. The true cost of customers is quite high. See for yourself. Add your total spending on all marketing including promotions, advertising, public relations, and sales departments: everything you spend to acquire customers. Then divide that by the actual number of net customers you get. Replacement customers don't count in this calculation. Most companies divide by total new customers, but this obscures the fact that many new customers are merely replacements for the customers you drove away. We use the net figure because the replacement customers only maintain your revenue. They don't increase revenue. The cost to acquire a net new customer is pretty scary for most companies. Many times that cost is greater than the additional revenues a truly new customer brings in.

Some studies have indicated that companies spend ten times as much trying to attract new customers as they spend trying to retain the customers they already have. For example, a company that refuses an exchange on a defective item will lose that customer who will leave and complain about the company to anyone who will listen. To attract a new customer, that same company will spend ten times the price of the defective product on advertising and promotions to replace that customer. Think about it in practical terms. Joe Customer buys a widget from your company. He takes it home and three days later it fails to function. He returns it to your business and your customer service employee takes it back and hands him a brand new one with an apology for his trouble. Joe Customer is not only satisfied, he tells everyone what a bargain he got because of the way your company stood behind his widget. You have not only kept a customer; you have also been the beneficiary of advertising you could never buy, and it has made it that much easier to turn new prospects into new customers-retail customers. It cost you only the wholesale price of the replacement product. It just does not make sense for a company to spend more money on gaining new customers when they overlook the advantages of spending on customer satisfaction and retention.

Playing the Numbers Game

An important point often overlooked in trying to replace new customers for those who have been chased away is simply the net numbers. Let's say that a company has lost 100 customers and has to advertise or run promotions to get new customers. If that advertising brings in 100 new people, the company does not have 100 new customers, it has 100 replacement customers. To net 100 new customers, the advertising, promotions, and discounts must bring in 200 new people. On the other hand, if the original 100 customers had been retained, the 100 new people are actually new customers. Spending enormous amounts of money that only brings in replacement customers for the ones that were lost does not mean any kind of growth.

Every dollar spent on customer service could mean approximately $10 saved on new customer acquisition. Therefore, it should be a financial no-brainer simply to take good care of your existing customers. Doing that is good for your brand, good for your company's reputation, good for employee morale, and good for your profits. There is also the goodwill generated within the community. Excellent customer service not only increases the financial performance of the company, it is just the right thing to do. Making customers happy is the reason why you are in business. Making them happy is much more than taking their money and saying "Have a nice day," as they walk out the door. Making them happy is the highest form of service for your organization.

It's easy to think your company is masterful at customer service when everything is going well. You sell the product, the customer is happy, and the experience is good for both the customer and you. The test of excellent customer service is what you do when everything possible goes wrong—the product does not work, the serviceman does not show up, the shipment is late, the model is wrong, or the phone call was not returned. Those are the times that really test your company's commitment to excellent customer service. It is these situations that build your customer service reputation. The character of your employees and the character of your company are truly revealed when things go wrong and your company is able to make them right.

The ECS Mindset

The company that is seriously working at retaining customers by providing excellent customer service has a different mindset about problems. This type of company welcomes the opportunity to satisfy an unhappy customer and make things right. The company recognizes that the cost of making the customer happy is miniscule compared to the cost of trying to replace him. This doesn't mean that a company actually wants problems to occur. A company like this simply understands that sooner or later something *will* go wrong. It stands willing and ready to remedy the problem. The problem is seen as an opportunity and employees are trained how to handle those opportunities.

> *"The test of excellent customer service is what you do when everything possible goes wrong..."*

Employees who work for companies where they know management is not going to do anything for an unhappy customer, dread having to deal with that customer. Management is upstairs in cozy, comfortable offices while the employee on the floor is in the direct line of fire. By contrast, the employee who knows the company will make every effort to make a customer happy and has been empowered to do whatever is possible, will enjoy dealing with the customer. Employees feel empowered when they have the authority to solve a problem for someone else. Employees almost always want to do the right thing for the customer. In many companies they are prevented from satisfying the customer by corporate policies and procedures. When employees have empathy for the customers but are not supported by the company, the employees will leave.

Customers notice the difference in the corporate attitude and philosophy when they receive excellent company service. The face of that employee, eager to be of service or handle a complaint, becomes the face of the company in the customer's mind. This is especially important when dealing with customer complaints. People who have a complaint or problem often come in with a combative mindset. A smiling, eager face and a helpful attitude diffuse a potentially bad situation.

When management has an ECS mindset, and when that mindset is understood and practiced by every person within the organization, the company becomes unstoppable. ECS becomes part of the company brand. That is because ECS becomes a part of what the company is known for throughout the industry, the customer base, and the community. As a result, ECS becomes a differentiator, setting the company apart from its competition. It gives a company a competitive advantage because customers are looking for that complete customer experience, but they so rarely get it. Obviously, then, ECS is a strategic imperative for any company wishing to be a leader in its market. No gimmick or business fad can produce the results that are inherent in implementing excellent customer service. It does not require a huge investment in new hardware or software. It may require some additional training, but it does not require a reengineering of the company. ECS is basically just a mindset, an attitude, a philosophy of service that, when filtered down throughout the company, focuses on the real reason for being in business—the customer.

Seek and Find; Ask and Be Answered

Managers I have worked with have asked me many times how they can know what will make customers happy. I often tell them this story I read once:

> *I was returning to the United States after a business trip to Southeast Asia. The flight was a long one, but when I arrived at Heathrow in London, there was an additional four hour delay. By the time I*

finally boarded the next airplane to continue my trip, I was already worn out and still had to cross the Atlantic to get to New York.

Normally, I fall asleep on flights, but on this occasion I simply could not get comfortable enough to sleep. Instead, I watched the onboard TV and did some reading. In New York I had a two-hour layover to connect with my American Airlines flight to Dallas, Texas. The moment I sat down on that plane, I leaned back and fell into a deep sleep.

Near the end of my flight, I awoke and began to stir a little. The man seated next to me started up a conversation and then said, "They served us a light meal but you were so sound asleep they passed you by." I replied, "I'm grateful that they did." Then I told him about my long flight and how exhausted I had been when I boarded the flight.

When the plane landed and we got up to leave, that man put on his jacket and I noticed an American Airlines pin on his lapel. Out of curiosity I asked him about the pin. It was then that he told me he worked for the airline, and it was his job to listen to passengers' opinions about the service. Needless to say, I was impressed by American's commitment to customer satisfaction. That experience made me book many more flights with American Airlines. That was twenty years ago, but I still have that excellent service image in my mind about the company.

There is the answer. If you want to know what customers want, ask them and listen intently to their answers. If a customer, for example, comes with a complaint, he or she will tell you what's wrong. But he won't or can't tell you what would make it right. Instead of memorizing special customer service scripts, simply ask him what it would take to make him happy.

Unless the demands of the customer are truly outrageous, at this point an employee empowered to do so may be able to solve the problem right there on the spot. If the demands are impossible to meet (you cannot supply the moon and the stars), the conversation does not stop there. Calmly tell him that your company cannot do the thing he requests. You ask what else you can do to make him happy.

Most people who come with a complaint will ask for one of two things—an exchange or a refund. These are reasonable requests that everyone has probably made at one time or another. Other customers may surprise you by asking for very little. At any rate, when the customer either receives what was demanded or some alternative that is within the limits of what can be done, a previously unhappy customer has been satisfied. The customer entered upset and vulnerable, expecting rejection and a verbal fight, but you took care of the situation. That customer leaves satisfied and is now a loyal customer who will return again and again. That customer has become an advocate for your business who will brag to acquaintances about the great service he or she got at your business. I am amazed that managers are willing to lose a customer, the customer's referrals, and create a lot of ill will all for the purchase price. But then, these same managers will approve multi-million dollar ad budgets to bring new customers in the front door. One more time: spending money to keep current customers is far cheaper than spending money to get new customers.

Bring Back the Past

Excellent customer service is nothing new. Long ago we called it standing behind your product. As business became more sophisticated, the same concept was called service after the sale. In any case, it was considered an integral part of the total sales experience. Now business consultants like me who are experts in customer service use the nomenclature of excellent customer service and total customer experience. It is all the same thing. The idea is to give the customer a satisfying experience from first impression to…well, to forever.

If you think about it, that idea is even more important today because of the rapid changes in technology that have taken place over the last few decades. Since the introduction of the transistor, things have changed rapidly. There was a time when an individual could buy and replace a tube that had gone out in the television set. There was a time when a person could make all of the minor repairs on the family automobile. Those days are gone forever. The new products are too technical, the materials too exotic, and even if they could, people are too busy to resolve problems with their purchases. Shade tree mechanics disappeared when automobiles needed to be hooked up to a diagnostic computer to do any repair work. Homeowners do fewer repairs themselves anymore. People are more dependent on suppliers and professionals for the goods and services they need to purchase. The bottom line is that more than ever, customers are dependent on companies to take care of them.

There When Needed

Excellent customer service means that the company will be on the spot when needed. For the same reason that home repairs are no longer viable, the customer needs expert help before the point of sale. Just looking at a row of laptop computers in an electronics store, for example, can be mind boggling. Most people need someone to explain the differences in the various models and which ones best suit the purpose they have in mind for its use. They literally *need* someone expert in the field to do that. Likewise, when something goes wrong with the computer, they *need* expert advice and service.

As an example, look at the history of Dell Computers. From the beginning, Dell's business model was simple: (1) receive an order for a computer with payment in full; (2) order the parts needed to build the computer paying the suppliers net 30; (3) within two weeks, ship the computer to the customer. You paid up front for the components before Dell ever received them. No risk for Dell. The computers were good but not really state-of-the-art. On top of that, Dell was telling customers in a culture of "I want it right now" that they should give the company their money and then wait two weeks for delivery. Dell even made customers prepay the shipping. Yet customers loved Dell for its reliability and its service. They bought so many Dell computers that the company became the number one computer manufacturer. Michael Dell, founder and CEO, became a billionaire. How was this possible? It wasn't the products. It certainly wasn't immediate gratification. The answer: it was simply the best customer service in the computer industry.

Sure, it was quicker and simpler just to go and buy a computer off the shelf in a store. But heaven help you if it malfunctioned. You were usually left to contact the manufacturer yourself.   The manufacturer, involved in building rather than repairing its computers, looked to the retailer to take care of most customer problems. Dell was different. Its customer service technicians actually answered their phones. They could often diagnose and solve whatever the problem was and ship out the replacement parts immediately. If the customer could not solve the problem by doing it himself, Dell dispatched a technician to solve the problem. Dell's aim was to make the customers happy by taking care of them. They were available 24/7 whenever the customer needed them. That business model paid off handsomely for Dell.

Making Things Right

On a more personal level, I have taken my family to the Chili's chain of restaurants on a number of occasions. The restaurants are clean, the food is decent, and the prices reasonable. But there have been a number of visits when something went wrong. Several times, the restaurant had run out of an already ordered dish. Once, the waitress spilled tea on my mother-in-law. Another time, they had run out of chocolate syrup for a dessert I had ordered. Each time they goofed up they would give me a card for a free dessert during a future visit. At one time I had such a stack of these cards that it became a running joke in our family. But, we continued to dine at Chili's. Today, Chili's is still one of our favorite family restaurants. Here's why:

In every case when something went wrong, the manager would come to our table to confirm the problem, and then personally apologize for the incident. In addition to the free dessert card, the staff would do whatever they could to make it right. Several times, my meal was complimentary. When they had no chocolate syrup for my dessert, they sent someone to the grocery to get some more syrup! (I found out because it seemed to be taking quite a while to serve a relatively simple dessert).

Neither the food nor the service was always perfect, but the staff intentions were good. When things went wrong, they did everything possible to make us happy. You have to like and admire people like that. We did, and I still do.

The Power of an Apology

Do not underestimate the power of an apology. Too often, we are told that the problem is not someone's responsibility, the customer's problem belongs to someone else's department, or that company policy is "blah, blah, blah". That's the same as saying that it is company policy NOT to make you happy. Regardless, whenever things go wrong and your customer is unhappy, it is a kindness to tell the customer that you are sorry this problem or bad experience occurred. Saying you're sorry this happened is not saying it's your fault. It is NOT saying you are responsible for the problem.

It is saying that you wished this had not happened to them. If you care at all about other people; if you care at all about your company's customers, you ARE sorry it happened. Say so. Then take the next step and do whatever you can to make it better. It doesn't have to be your fault for you to make it better, or to make it right. Try it the next time you have an unhappy customer. The customer will feel so much better, and so will you.

What the Best are Doing

Recently *Business Week* magazine inaugurated an annual list of the 25 best companies for customer service. Included in the article were outstanding examples of corporate understanding of what it takes to make customers happy. Here are a few of them:

- A businessman traveling on Southwest Airlines got caught in a tangle of delays caused by the weather and FAA flight regulations. His flight was delayed on the runway for 4 ½ hours. During that time, he was amazed that the pilot and crew walked the aisles, answered questions, and looked as though they really cared. On top of that, he later received a letter of apology from the airline and vouches for two round trip tickets. It is easy to see why Southwest's handling of a bad situation brought nothing but praise from an inconvenienced passenger.

- Four Seasons Hotels understands that the employees need to experience first hand the service and accommodations in order to understand the customer's needs. From housekeepers to department managers, the hotel provides free stays in their luxury hotels with the proviso that they fill out forms describing their experiences during their stay. The hotel looks on this as a training expense, giving the staff a personal taste of what it is like to be on the other side of the hotel's service.

- Toyota Motor's attention to personal service for Lexus owners is considered a part of the price of the cars and has become the industry leader in such service.

- Some businesses like Ritz-Carlton Hotels are actively involved in improving service even though it is already superior to that of their competition. They understand that complacency is never a part of excellent customer service.

As more companies like these recognize the importance of ECS and implement better programs, those companies who neglect ECS are headed for extinction. In business it is wise to realize that the customer truly *is* king, and the king should get exactly what he wants.

ECS: A Summary

Customer service is a key component to the overall brand. It is not just a single transaction, however. It is every contact the customer has with your business. The simple question everyone in your organization should ask is, "How difficult is it to do business with our company?"

Look over these areas as a checklist:
1. **Is the order form** easy to fill out accurately or does it confuse many people who try to use it?

2. **Is our website** easy to navigate when searching out our products? Is it easy to order and pay for items in the shopping cart?

3. **Could we improve** on our delivery methods?

4. **How friendly and helpful** is our phone presence—information, tech support, or sales conversations?

5. **Do we keep ample inventory** so that customers do not have to wait for the products they want?

6. **Are our showrooms** laid out rationally and conveniently? Do we schedule restocking at low traffic times or after hours?

7. **What do our salespeople look like** when they meet face to face with customers? Are they clean cut and dressed appropriately?

8. **Are our marketing materials** well put together, easy to read, and attractive?

9. **Do the warranties we offer** really amount to an added value to the product?

10. **How do we go about problem resolution** so that the customer feels as though we really care?

11. **Are our refund policies** fair and uncomplicated?

12. **What system for dispute resolution** do we have in place, and is it equitable and transparent?

Anything that involves interaction with customers is part of customer service. Every area of that contact must be examined for flaws in order to achieve Excellent Customer Service.

It is my hope as a business consultant that the principles laid out in this book will change the thinking of business owners and executives everywhere. Whatever systems or programs management puts into place for the product or business operations should always be secondary to the company's true purpose: serving our customers and making their lives better.

Keys to this Chapter

The purpose of business is to satisfy the wants and needs of customers. Profit is the result and the reward for being of service to customers.

Treat your employees well, but customers are the top priority.

Excellent customer service gives you a competitive advantage because so few companies provide it.

The best way to please a dissatisfied customer is simply to ask him what it will take to make him happy.

Satisfying an unhappy customer will enhance your image, save you money, and create an ambassador who will refer other customers.

7 Keys to Higher Profits, Happier Employees, and More Satisfied Customers

1. Choose executives for their leadership, not their Greedership.

2. Remember that the purpose of the organization is to serve the customers. Profit is the reward for good service.

3. Management fads come and go. Taking care of people always works.

4. Mergers are distractions that rarely work out. Do what you do best.

5. Layoffs are a short-term fix for a long-term problem. Find the real problem and fix it.

6. You can't downsize your way to prosperity. Downsizing just turns a large dysfunctional company into a smaller dysfunctional company.

7. Spend more on customer retention, and you can spend less on customer acquisition. It's also cheaper to keep your current customers than it is to buy new ones.

About the Author

Alan Stafford is a professional speaker, organizational development consultant, and executive coach. As President of Stafford Speaking and Consulting, he travels the United States showing companies how to develop effective leaders, create productive teams, and deliver legendary customer service. Alan does this through keynote speeches, seminars, workshops, and corporate retreats. More than an entertaining speaker, he delivers real value that attendees can use immediately on the job and at home.

Most Popular Programs
Developing Effective Leaders
Building Teams that Get Along and Get things Done
Legenary Customer Service as a Competitive Advantage
A New Way to Manage and Motivate People
Branding's Not Just for Cowboys

His consults with companies on communications, business relationships, and customer service/retention, and coaches executives on leadership issues, personal productivity, and personal relationships. Alan has an MBA and an MHA, and is a Fellow of the American College of Healthcare Executives. Despite his strong background in healthcare and technology, he speaks to and consults for companies in all industries and sectors. Alan is also a certified coach who mentors other coaches, and is an instructor for a major coaching school.

ORDER FORM FOR THIS BOOK
Making Companies Work

To order by:

Telephone:	866-200-3888
Fax:	704-788-6694
Email:	orders@eplanetpublishing.com
Internet:	www.eplanetpublishing.com
Mail:	ePlanet Publishing, Inc.
	109025 David Taylor Drive
	Suite 100
	Charlotte, NC 28262

Name _____

Address _____

City _____ State _____ Zip _____

Phone _____

Email _____

Please send me _____ copies of Making Companies Work at $26.95
        Plus $5.95 Shipping and Handling in the U.S.

Total $_____

☐ Check ☐ Money Order ☐ Visa ☐ MasterCard ☐ AMEX

Card Number _____

Name on Card _____

Exp _____ Security Code _____

Prices subject to change without notice.
Call or email us for quantity pricing.